FRONTIER ELEGANCE:

The Early Architecture of Walpole, New Hampshire 1750 - 1850

by Bill Ranauro

Bill Ranauro

5-2-19

Frontier Elegance
Copyright © 2019 by Bill Ranauro

Published by Piscataqua Press
An imprint of RiverRun Bookstore, Inc.
32 Daniel Street
Portsmouth, NH 03801
www.riverrunbookstore.com
www.piscataquapress.com

ISBN: 978-1-790702-32-9

Printed in the United States of America.

BY THE SAME AUTHOR

West of Boston:
Growing Up Red Sox in a Yankee Household
(memoir)

For the citizens of Walpole

Contents

Appendices:

INTRODUCTION

Located fifteen miles north of Keene, New Hampshire, on the banks of the Connecticut River and in the shadow of Fall Mountain, the town of Walpole has developed and maintained a rich and diverse architectural heritage. While several fine houses from Walpole's frontier beginnings in the mid-eighteenth century still stand, the town's best architectural period is represented by the outstanding collection of Federal Period and Greek Revival houses that dot its picturesque landscape. Worthy examples from the late eighteenth and early nineteenth centuries can be found throughout the town, though Walpole village provides a concentration of structures that will be the focus of this study (see Table 1.1). Indeed, it is in this area that the town's architectural character was first developed and is today best represented.

To put Walpole's early architecture in a proper historical context, it seems worthwhile to trace the roots of architectural style that emerged in New England and, of particular interest to Walpole, the Connecticut Valley. This would include an examination of the people who created these houses, as well as the influences that came to bear on their designs.

Additionally, it is of interest to uncover the extent to which Walpole's architecture corresponded with the wider stylistic trends of the late eighteenth and early nineteenth centuries. To be sure, Walpole was a part of the frontier upon its first settlement in this period, and was still very much a part of the rural hinterland as late as the first half of the nineteenth century. The designs of prominent architects were in evidence in other places throughout New England, and their influence would be felt through the printing and use of architectural pattern books by local builders. This would be perhaps the single most important factor in the emerging architecture of the Connecticut River Valley and in Walpole over the first half-century or so of America's existence as a nation. Also, the local crafts community, as well as the owners of these houses would bring their own influence to bear. In any case, it's likely that

Table 1.1: Select List of Important
Early Buildings in Walpole

House/Structure	Period/Style	Date of Construction
Walpole-Bellows Inn	Colonial/Georgian	1762
Historic House	Dutch Colonial Saltbox	1761
Tatum-Peck House	Georgian/Federal	1792
Bellows-Grant House	Georgian w/Federal and Greek details	1792/1840s
Watkins Tavern	Georgian/Federal	1792
Knapp House	Federal	1812
Porter House	Greek Revival	1790/1840
Walpole Academy	Greek Revival	1831
Bemis-Howland House	Greek Revival	1833
Wing House	Greek Revival	1840
Buffum House	Georgian/Greek Revival	1785/1835
Howland-Schofield House	Greek/Gothic Revival	1844
Roentsch House	Colonial Revival	1915

Walpole's citizens were eager to achieve a degree of sophistication and status through the local interpretation of the most current architectural styles coming to them from England by way of Boston and lower Connecticut River Valley communities such as New Haven, Connecticut, and Northampton, Massachusetts.

The people of Walpole, like other New England communities from this time-period, would have been concerned with how various factors would help shape public virtue and the public good. On speaking of the moral influence of good houses, the nineteenth-century architectural theorist and critic Andrew Jackson Downing said, "…there is a moral influence in a country home – when, among an educated, truthful, and refined people, it is an echo of their character – which is more powerful than any mere oral teachings of virtue and morality."[1] Though Downing's taste leaned more toward the Gothic Revival of the mid-nineteenth century and less toward the classical style that dominated the early architecture of Walpole, his point was that the family home could be seen as a direct expression of order and fulfillment in life.

Indeed, Walpole provides a powerful example of how individuals within a community can come together to achieve a degree of grace, distinction, and moral standing through their buildings. Just as a work of art or literature is capable of functioning as an expression of community values and tastes, so too can architecture transmit similar qualities and judgments. To what degree the houses of Walpole were an indication of their inhabitants' status and place in the community is of importance here as well.

---

[1] A.J. Downing, *The Architecture of Country Houses* (New York: Dover Publications, Inc., 1969), xix-xx. (Reprint of original 1850 publication)

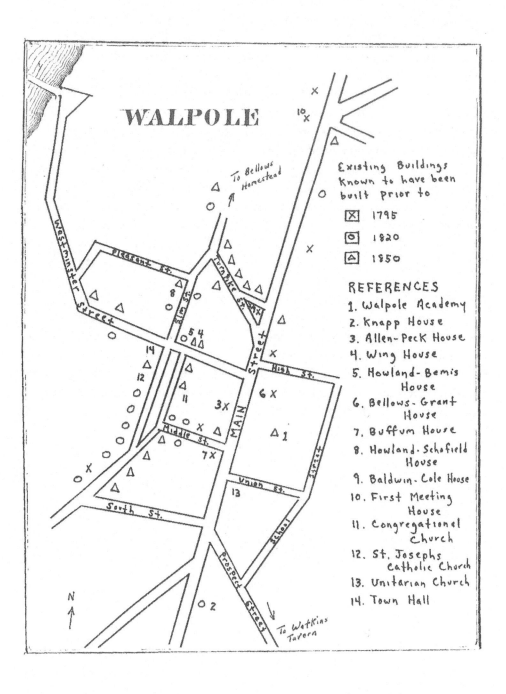

WALPOLE

To Bellows
Homestead

Existing Buildings
Known to have been
built prior to

⊠ 1795
⊙ 1820
△ 1850

REFERENCES
1. Walpole Academy
2. Knapp House
3. Allen-Peck House
4. Wing House
5. Howland-Bemis
      House
6. Bellows-Grant
      House
7. Buffum House
8. Howland-Schofield
      House
9. Baldwin-Cole House
10. First Meeting
      House
11. Congregational
      Church
12. St. Josephs
      Catholic Church
13. Unitarian Church
14. Town Hall

Westminster Street
Pleasant St.
Kingman St.
Turnpike St.
Main Street
High St.
Middle St.
Union St.
School Street
South St.
Prospect Street

To Watkins
Tavern

N

PART I

THE WIDER VIEW:
ITALY, ENGLAND AND THE
TRANSMISSION OF STYLE
TO NEW ENGLAND

CHAPTER 1

Frontier Beginnings

Walpole, which had its beginnings in 1736 as a grant by the Massachusetts General Court (New Hampshire being considered a part of the Massachusetts Bay Colony until 1741), was not chartered until 1752 when Colonel Benjamin Bellows (1712–1777) obtained a charter from the colonial governor Benning Wentworth. Among the privileges afforded by the charter, Bellows was given the authority to make grants of land to prospective settlers. Colonial authorities, including Governor Wentworth, were undoubtedly eager to attract settlers to the sparsely populated western regions of the colony. However, the threat of hostile Native Americans in the region brought significant risk to settlers.

Benjamin Bellows was a noted land surveyor who had come from Lunenburg, Massachusetts to settle on the New Hampshire side of the Connecticut River, moving his family to Walpole a year later in 1753. A makeshift fort sufficed for the first years, since the aforementioned threat of Indians was very real in this period. Nancy Heffernan comments that "scarcely any family escaped the effects of sudden house burnings, scalping, slaughter, captivity, and looting…"[1] This threat, together with the uncertainties of life in such a remote location on the outskirts of civilization, made survival a challenge.

As might be expected under the circumstances, settlement was slow. A resident reported that by 1762, there were "about twelve to fifteen houses in town."[2] Other settlers moved in slowly, and by the time of the first census in 1767, 308 people were recorded as living in the town (see Fig. 4). By the beginning of the American Revolution almost a decade later, a militia force of

---

[1] Nancy Coffey Heffernan and Ann Page Stecker, *New Hampshire: Crosscurrents in Its Development* (Grantham, NH: Tompson and Ruuter Inc., 1986), 83.
[2] Martha M. Frizzell, *A History of Walpole, New Hampshire, Vol. I* (The Vermont Printing Co., 1963), 8.

thirty-five men would answer the call to arms at Lexington. The group was led by Benjamin Bellows II (1740 – 1802), son of the original grantee. The junior Bellows would later acquire the title of "General" Benjamin Bellows.

From this earliest period of Walpole's existence, two houses of note survive, having stood for more than 265 years. The town's grantee, Colonel Benjamin Bellows, built what was likely the grandest and most substantial house to be found for many miles around. Bellows had waited almost ten years from the town's founding to build this house, likely because of the previously mentioned threat of Indians in the region. It was not until this threat had abated following the end of the French and Indian War in 1761 that it was safe to proceed with building outside the fort they had been living in prior to this time.[3]

Walpole was essentially the wilderness in the 1760s, so a house of ample size and stature would have been rare in the upper Connecticut Valley in this period. It seems clear that, by constructing this house, Bellows was making a statement about his leading place in the town. The Bellows Homestead (1762), which retains many of the architectural details of the mid-eighteenth century Georgian style (see chapter 2), remains standing today as the Bellows-Walpole Inn (Fig.1). The two and one-half stories, symmetrical façade with centered door, five-bay window arrangement, and gambrel roof with dormers, were all features typical of colonial houses of substance built after about 1750.

Despite the early date of the Bellows Homestead, another house in Walpole village may slightly predate this structure. The house on North Main Street today, known simply as the "Historic House" (1761), ranks as the oldest standing structure in Walpole (Fig.2). Walpole resident Ray Boas tells the story of how the house barely escaped demolition in 1930.[4] When an oil company intended to buy the property for the purpose of constructing a filling station, a number of concerned citizens were stirred to action to save the house. A loan was obtained and the property was purchased with the purpose of making it the headquarters of the newly formed Walpole Historical Society (WHS). This plan was successful and in fact the house would display the collections of the WHS until 1948.

This house combines a saltbox in the rear with a gambrel roofline in the front. The bottom section of the gambrel roof employs an unusual convex, or pulvinated, roofline leading to the eaves, and acts as a covering for the

---

[3] In the years between 1744 and 1760, northern New England had been a battle-ground in the struggle for North America between France and England. Hostilities ceased in 1761, though the Treaty of Paris would not be signed until 1763.
[4] Ray Boas, "Did You Know That…? Excursions into Walpole People, Places & History with Ray Boas," *The Walpole Clarion* (Vol. VIII, Issue 5, April 2018), 14.

FIG.1 BELLOWS HOMESTEAD, built in 1762 by the grantee of Walpole, Colonel Benjamin Bellows

FIG.2 HISTORIC HOUSE, WALPOLE, 1761. This house remains as the oldest standing structure in Walpole

FIG.3 HISTORIC HOUSE, profile of the north side of the house shows the unusual roof line, employing a salt box in back with a gambrel in front. The curved bottom is seen in a house in Woodbury, Connecticut

columned front porch (Fig.3). This feature is more commonly tied to the Dutch Colonial, a style rarely seen in New England and more common to the Hudson River Valley of New York state.[5] However, examples of this type which date to the eighteenth century survive today in Woodbury and Essex, Connecticut.[6] Considering that many of Walpole's early residents migrated up the Connecticut River Valley to New Hampshire and Vermont, these eighteenth century Connecticut structures may have been the inspiration for this early Walpole home, which today serves as a private residence.

[5] John Milnes Baker, *American House Styles: A Concise Guide* (New York: The Countryman Press, 2018), 104. Baker goes on to say that "Scholars do not agree whether the characteristic roof of this style was an adaptation of a Flemish farm house or was an original type developed here as an amalgamation of several colonial building patterns borrowed from the English."
[6] Samuel Chamberlain, *A Small House in the Sun: The Visage of Rural New England in Photographs* (New York: Hastings House, 1936/1971), 48-49.

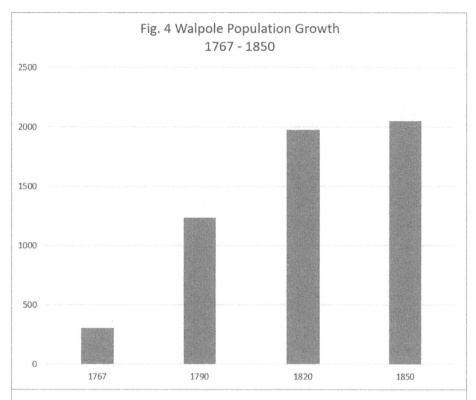

Fig. 4 Walpole Population Growth
1767 - 1850

Source: George Aldrich, *Walpole As It Was and As It Is.* Claremont, NH: Claremont Manufacturing Co., 1880.

Indeed, both the Walpole-Bellows Inn and the "Historic House" on North Main Street have undergone extensive and meticulous renovation in recent years. These two houses, though unique in their style, scale, and purpose, were mostly typical of the architecture that predated the Federal, or Adam style that would predominate in Walpole and elsewhere in New England after about 1790.

Despite the slow start, Walpole grew fairly rapidly following the end of the French and Indian War. After the first census was taken in 1767, steady growth was recorded until about 1820, when the population leveled off (Fig. 4). As the grantee, Bellows was responsible for deeding tracts of land to new settlers. Town historian Martha Frizzell tells us that by the time of the first census, the population was already beginning to center in the present day village. This area supplies us with many fine examples of architecturally significant buildings from the late eighteenth and early nineteenth centuries. A factor promoting this pattern of settlement and building was the location of the first meeting house on North Main Street (see map). It should be noted that Bellows had intended the village to develop closer to his own house, about one-half mile north of the present day village.[7]

A look at the map further supports the idea that the village quickly became a vibrant center of economic, political, and social activity. Upon seeing Walpole in the earliest years of the nineteenth century, Timothy Dwight, president of Yale University and an indefatigable New England traveler, noted Walpole's important geographical location, and hence its important economic role: "As this is the principal channel of communication between Boston and the country on the northwest, the traveling and transportation on it are great. This village has become the seat of considerable business, and contains a printing office and a bookstore."[8]

Indeed, Dwight's observations would foreshadow Walpole's role as a center of literary and cultural activity. In 1797 writer David Carlisle opened a print shop on Main Street, thus opening one of the more interesting chapters in Walpole's history. Four years previously, the *Farmer's Weekly Museum* was established by Carlisle and Isaiah Thomas, whom Carlisle had apprenticed under in Worcester, Massachusetts. Joseph Dennie served as editor and would take over the paper in 1796. Sometime after 1797, Carlisle moved the print shop into the Buffum house.[9]

Although the paper was apparently not an immediate success, it began a literary tradition in Walpole which would remain for some time.[10] One result of the paper being published in Walpole was the corps of talented writers and critics who were drawn to the town. Numbering among these authors were Royal Tyler, a lawyer of some wit and later Chief Justice of Vermont; Samuel Hunt, who afterwards became a member of Congress; Samuel West of Keene, a prolific writer, as well as David Everett, Thomas Green Fessendon, Isaac

---

[7] Frizzell, 15.

[8] Thea Wheelwright and Katharine Knowles, *Travels in New England* (New York: Bonanza Books, 1989), 72.

[9] See chapter 6 for a description of this important house in Walpole history.

[10] Walpole citizens can look back at a long line of prominent writers and cultural figures who have populated the town over time. These would include, to name a few, the aforementioned Joseph Dennie, Royal Tyler, and their many colleagues among "The Wits"; the transcendentalist Bronson Alcott; his daughter, the popular novelist Louisa May Alcott; author James Michener, who established a connection with the town in his best-selling novel *Hawaii*; present-day writer and historian Dayton Duncan; and documentary filmmaker Ken Burns.

Story and others.[11] The dry, routine news snatches of the paper's early days gave way by 1796 to poems, essays, criticism, and political commentary. By 1800, the *Farmer's Weekly Museum* was clearly "of the Federal Stripe"[12] and had established itself as one of New England's finest weeklies.

This collection of literary figures who wrote for the *Farmer's Weekly Museum* all belonged to a literary club known as the "Society of Wits," or simply as the "Walpole Wits." It was not uncommon to find the Wits engaged in late-night merrymaking at one of the several inns and taverns in town. The Watkins Tavern (see chapter 4) sometimes served as their venue, but more often the group met at Crafts Tavern, which was situated closer to the print shop on Main Street. George Aldrich colorfully describes what might typically have taken place at one of their meetings:

> The old tavern, in those days, at those gatherings, was turned into a literary pandemonium; wine drinking, late suppers, card playing, joke cracking and the like formed the programme [*sic*] for frequent meetings during the year... The good cheer of Major Bullard's house (Crafts Tavern) was known far and wide, and all travelers wanting a good time made it a point to stop at the Major's.[13]

At the center of the "coterie of wags, wits, and literati,"[14] was the aforementioned Joseph Dennie. Dennie became known for his weekly essays from the "Lay Preacher." His writing brought a quality to the paper that inspired no less a personage than Nathaniel Hawthorne to quip that Dennie was at one time "the finest writer in America."[15]

It would seem rather unlikely that, as far back as the late eighteenth century, a remote outpost such as Walpole would develop as a center of literary activity and output. And in fact, after Dennie's departure in 1799, the quality of the paper fell off markedly. The *Farmer's Weekly Museum* was published on and off in Walpole until 1828 when operations were moved to Keene. The paper would be known as the *Cheshire Republican* from this date.

Walpole's early role as a literary and cultural center on the frontier was mirrored in its architectural development. William Hosley, in discussing the

---

[11] George Aldrich, *Walpole As It Was and as it Is* (Claremont, NH: Claremont Manu-facturing Co., 1880), 79.
[12] Aldrich, 80.
[13] Aldrich, 80.
[14] Aldrich, 81.
[15] Harold Milton Ellis, *Joseph Dennie and His Circle* (Austin: University of Texas, 1915), iii.

range of architectural styles in the Connecticut Valley following the American Revolution, i.e., after 1785, concluded that "northern towns like Walpole, New Hampshire, and Windsor, Vermont, developed into flourishing centers of trade and manufacturing."[16] Hosley introduces the idea that these northern towns, i.e., towns on the Connecticut River in New Hampshire and Vermont, were almost certainly built "by a new generation of house wrights and architects whose methods of work and more extensive use of pattern books bespeaks an increased level of professionalization in the building trade."[17]

Finally, we should know something about the people who lived in these houses. We can assume that often, though perhaps not always, the owner would be assisting the master builder or carpenter. Most men, though not all, would have possessed at least some carpentry skills, and would have been making decisions relative to the taste and details to be included on their house. Cost and available materials would likely have affected these decisions. As well, the houses being built in the eighteenth and nineteenth centuries, much as today, were an expression of a person's and family's status and place in the community.

---

[16] William N. Hosley, "Architecture," in *The Great River: Art and Society of the Connecticut Valley, 1635 – 1820,* ed. Gerald W.R. Ward and William N. Hosley (Hartford, CN: Wadsworth Museum, 1985), 66.

[17] Hosley, "Architecture," 66.

CHAPTER 2

Bulfinch, Benjamin, and the Federal Style in New England

When attempting to discuss architecture in a historical context, it is often convenient to apply stylistic labels to periods of time. Unfortunately, the labels commonly used are not always employed with a great deal of thought or accuracy, and can serve to confuse rather than clarify a building's origins. A common misnomer is the use of the term "Colonial," which is loosely applied by some to mean any house that strikes them as old. A story told by Michael Behrendt of Rochester, New Hampshire, illustrates the casual (and inaccurate) way in which this term is often used. A historic home in Rochester, built in 1882 in the Queen Anne style, was advertised by a local realtor as a "Colonial"![1] A comparison of houses built in the Colonial and Queen Anne styles would quickly disabuse the viewer of any similarity between the two styles. Similarly, architectural historian John Milnes Baker frustratingly laments the common mistake of assuming that buildings featuring columns are "colonial" in style: "The Greek Revival has persisted to this day in the mistaken notion that such a house is a colonial."[2] The Greek Revival is a style whose origins are decidedly from the nineteenth century.

In an architectural context the term "Colonial" literally refers to houses built prior to the American Revolution, i.e., before 1775, or perhaps as late as 1785.[3] The term "Georgian" is also used widely, and by some interchangeably

---

[1] Michael Behrendt, *The Architectural Jewels of Rochester, New Hampshire: A History of the Built Environment* (Charleston, SC: The History Press, 2009), 42.
[2] Baker, 46.
[3] The period of the American Revolution saw relatively little building in New England. It's fair to assume that building styles from 1775 to 1785 continued as they had from before the outbreak of hostilities.

with the term "Colonial." Presumably, the term "Georgian" is meant to refer to structures built during the successive reigns of four Kings of England by that name – George -- and spanning the years from 1714 to 1830, when King George IV died.[4] In practical terms, the use of the term Georgian in an architectural sense essentially disappears in America after the Revolution, that is, after about 1780. Hence, it seems fair to equate the term "Georgian" with "Colonial" when describing structures built in the eighteenth-century.

Part of the reason for this inaccurate usage is that the term "Georgian" is really meant as a dynastic, rather than as a stylistic term.[5] Because there would be a number of stylistic changes in architecture over the course of the reign of the House of Hanover in England, it is difficult to designate any one style or set of details and ornamentation as "Georgian" (see Table 2.1).

A more reasonable method of classifying architectural periods in America is to actually look at the factors inspiring style, ornament, and function in buildings. However, even this method can lead to confusion in rural areas like Walpole, where builders, whether by whim or necessity, would often cross over several defined periods of architecture on a single structure. Indeed, it's common to find in many of the early houses of Walpole the elements of both Georgian and Federal details together, as well as Federal and Greek Revival ornament and decoration on the same house. In at least one case, elements of the Gothic Revival are seen together with the Greek Revival. Examples of this broad-based approach to style will be discussed and illustrated in the second half of this book.

This eclecticism is due to several factors. First, in the eighteenth century, the transmission of the Georgian style moved from England to America largely via architecture books and carpenter's handbooks (see Appendix I). Outside of the more prosperous urban communities on the coast, such as Boston, Salem, Newport, and Portsmouth, the title of "professional architect" could hardly be claimed by any man in the colonies, so reliance on these sources was essential.

Perhaps the first man in America who would have remotely deserved the title of professional architect was Peter Harrison (1716-1775). Harrison is significant because he was instrumental in helping to popularize the classical

---

[4] William IV of Hanover, son of George III, would rule until his death in 1837, followed by Queen Victoria who would rule until 1901, thus bringing the ruling dynasty to an end in Britain.

[5] William H. Pierson, *American Buildings and Their Architects – Volume I: The Colonial and Neoclassical Styles* (New York: Oxford University Press, 1986), 111. See Appendix III for a timeline of architectural terms and styles in New England from 1600 to 1850.

Table 2.1: Second Period Architecture in America:
Georgian-Colonial Style, 1715 – 1780

Detail	Early Georgian (1715-1750)	High/Late Georgian (1750-1780)
Siding	• Wood framed; clapboard • Corners marked by angle quoins	• Sometimes rusticated • Corners often marked by giant pilasters
Doors	• Front door with rectangular transom window • Angular or scroll pediment	• Front door with semi-circular arched fan light • Segmental pediment over door
Roofs	• Steeply pitched roof • Multiple gables	• Lower roof pitch; hipped or gambrel roof line, frequently with dormers
Windows	• Dormers with rectangular windows • Windows with many small panes • Plain or corniced windows • Single arched window on stair landing	• Dormers with arched windows • Windows with fewer and larger panes • Window pediments • Palladian window more popular for stair landing

Source: Hugh Morrison, *Early American Architecture*, pp.316-317.

FIG.5 VILLA FOSCARI ("LA MALCONTENTA"), VENETO, ITALY, Andrea Palladio, 1560. This view is from the rear of the building. Note the large scale "Palladian Window"

Palladian style associated with the early Georgian period in America. John Milnes Baker points out Palladio's overwhelming influence in the development of architectural style, first in England, and later on in America. Acknowledged as the most important architect of the Italian Renaissance, Baker says of Palladio that "his country houses inland from Venice were unlike anything that had been built before. They would come to inspire generations of architects and scholars."[6] The Villa Foscari (1560), also known as "La Malcontenta," is typical of the country villas Palladio was commissioned to design by Italian patricians in the sixteenth century (Fig.5). Around 1620, the English statesman and architect Inigo Jones introduced the Palladian style in England following an extended stay in northern Italy in the early seventeenth century. After becoming popular in England, the Palladian style was brought to America via the handbooks previously cited.

The earliest example of the Palladian style in America is Harrison's facade

[6] Baker, 17.

of the Redwood Library (1748) in Newport, which may well have been inspired by Palladio's Church of Santo Giorgio Maggiore in Venice (Fig.6 and Fig.7).[7] The source for this inspiration was likely found in William Kent's *Designs of Inigo Jones,* a book that was found among Harrison's considerable library of architecture books. Among the other important and still-standing buildings of Peter Harrison's design are King's Chapel (1754), Boston, Christ Church (1761) in Cambridge, and Touro Synagogue (1763) of Newport.[8] Each of these buildings is considered a masterpiece of Georgian design. In any case, Harrison's (and others') extensive use of English architecture books points up the importance of these books in the transmission of the Georgian style across the Atlantic from England to the American colonies.

While standards of style were largely set in the coastal cities of New England, and were to varying degrees emulated in inland towns, rural communities such as Walpole would come to depend on local builder-architects. Author Hugh Morrison explains that:

> ...most buildings in the colonies were designed by owners and assisted by carpenter-builders, who together would lay out the elements of the plan and structure... Comparison of such features [doorways, mantel-pieces, windows, etc.] in existing houses with the engraved plates of the handbooks leaves little doubt about the specifics of many Georgian details. Yet it also reveals that the carpenters and joiners of the colonies departed freely – and usually intelligently – from their sources, altering a detail here or a dimension there in accordance with necessity, invention, or taste.[9]

Of course, this habit of modifying or departing from strict compliance with the plates of these handbooks would continue long after the American Revolution and well into the nineteenth-century. This would include handbooks that were later written by Americans, as well as the continuing influence of English architects (see again, Appendix I).

---

[7] Harrison employed a technique called "rustication" in the effort to create the appearance of stone masonry as the building material for the Redwood Library. Sand would be mixed with the paint covering the beveled wood exterior to create the effect of a roughened, stone surface.

[8] Carl Bridenbaugh, *Peter Harrison: First American Architect* (Chapel Hill: University of North Carolina Press, 1949), 182; fig. 15-18. Touro Synagogue, which continues to the present day as an active congregation, ranks as the oldest synagogue in America.

[9] Hugh Morrison, *Early American Architecture: From the First Settlements to the National Period* (New York: Dover Publications, 1987), 291.

FIG. 6 REDWOOD LIBRARY, NEWPORT by Peter Harrison,
Architect, 1748

FIG. 7 CHURCH OF SANTO GIORGIO MAGGIORE, VENICE,
by Andrea Palladio, c. 1570-1610

There is an additional factor that might explain the changes and modifications made by the original builders (and later owners) long after the original date of construction. For example, altering a doorway or façade to reflect a new trend or style, such as the Greek Revival, to a house originally built in the Federal style, was fairly common. This kind of change shows up in several houses in Walpole. Of course, function and ease of construction were factors which often took precedence over style and aesthetic considerations, but the influence of English architects could be seen rather quickly in America.

Since there were to be significant changes and alterations of style over the period from before the American Revolution, labeling all the architecture dating from before this time as "Georgian" then, would be misleading and inaccurate. It needs to be recognized that the forces and influences guiding architectural design from 1600 to about 1720 (often referred to as "First Period Architecture") were distinct from those after this time. This, of course, predates Walpole's settlement, and is limited to the coastal communities of New England. The introduction of certain stylistic changes such as those inspired by Palladio welcomed in a new era in English (and consequently American) architecture. This was the architecture of the previously mentioned Peter Harrison.

Palladianism generally emphasized balance and symmetry in the construction and design of buildings, and was a reaffirmation of classical principles, particularly as found in the work of the seventeenth-century Englishman Inigo Jones. "This," asserts architectural historian William Pierson, "was the first phase of Georgian architecture."[10] This is largely found in floor plans, window and door placement, and even in the placement of two end chimneys to replace the more traditional large central chimney. This period generally extends from 1720 to post-Revolutionary America, i.e., about 1785, and is alternately referred to as "Second-Period Architecture." The first houses built in Walpole were from this period.

Hugh Morrison points out that the development of the Georgian style was one of gradual evolution rather than sudden change.[11] Therefore, it should be noted that, in looking at Second-Period architecture, a broad distinction can be found between early and later Georgian architecture. Most of the changes occur somewhere around mid-century (see Table 2.1). Walpole's first homes were built in the latter part of this period and retain at least some elements of

---

[10] Pierson, 112.
[11] Morison, 316.

the style and taste of Palladian design.[12] These include the aforementioned "Historic House" (Fig.2) located in the current-day village on North Main Street, and especially the Walpole-Bellows Inn (Fig.1). Of course, Palladio's influence did not totally evaporate after this time, and certain aspects of his influence would in fact continue well into the nineteenth-century.

The changes in style and taste following 1785 came during America's formative years as a nation, and inspired the desire for an architecture that would reflect the values of the new nation. Known as the "Federal Style," this architecture represents a period in American history when our federal system of government was being developed. Despite America's political independence from England, this new style of architecture was highly influenced by Robert Adam, Britain's most popular and influential architect of the eighteenth century. Adam, who was from Edinburgh, Scotland originally but settled in London to work, was highly inspired by both Greek and Roman forms, which American architects and builders enthusiastically embraced.[13] Adam became familiar with these forms and details on a four-year tour of Italy in the 1740s.[14] Rather than spend his time carousing with the aristocracy (as his brother James unashamedly did) while in Italy, Adam would become intensely engaged in study, making drawings, sketches, and moldings of all the architectural details he saw. It was during this time that he developed the theoretical and practical basis for the architectural style that would become associated with his name.[15]

The Federal, or "Adam" style as it is sometimes called, would begin after the Revolution in America and would predominate until about 1825. As mentioned, Adam acquired his knowledge and taste for classical architectural forms and details as a result of his four-year Grand Tour of Italy and the Dalmatian coast. In contrast to the Palladian style that was based on the great villas and temples created by Palladio almost 200 years before, Adam's studies influenced him to adopt the philosophy that "Roman domestic architecture

---

[12] For example, the Bellows Homestead (1762) retains the gambrel style roof associated with this period. Buildings of Neoclassical design (after 1785) will see the virtual elimination of gambrel rooflines, and the introduction of lower pitched gable and hip style roofs.

[13] Bruce Wentworth, "Ask the Architect: 'Federal'" *Ask the Architect* www.askthearchitect.org accessed May 24, 2017.

[14] Often referred to as the "Grand Tour," a stay in Italy to study its ancient ruins and art became a requirement for eighteenth-century English gentlemen looking to finish their education. Unlike most of the young English aristocrats who wasted much of their time in the parlors of Italian patricians, Robert Adam utilized his time wisely in learning his craft.

[15] Doreen Yarwood, *Robert Adam* (New York: Charles Scribner's Sons, 1970), 49-88.

should be more suitable as a basis for designing English homes than Classical temples."[16]

As his practice in London matured, Adam further indicated that "a great architect should not hesitate to alter the classical rules of proportion and detail if, by so doing, he could interpret more accurately and with spirit the essence of the classical order."[17] Adam's observations while in Italy convinced him that this flexible attitude regarding detail and decoration is what the ancient Greeks and Romans believed in. Interestingly, this is exactly the opposite of what English Palladianism had become, with its strict adherence to rigid, unbending rules. What was new then, was that Adam used Roman motifs consistently in the service of a philosophy of design that placed sensibility and visual effect above "the rules."[18] Upon returning to London after his travels in the late 1740s, Adam would spend the next four decades transforming the architecture of that city.

The person perhaps most responsible for America's adherence to Adam's Neoclassical style was the Bostonian Charles Bulfinch (1763-1844). After taking the Grand Tour of the European capitals of London, Paris, and Rome between 1785 and 1787, Bulfinch returned to Boston determined to unseat the austere and strict Palladianism that had dominated Boston and New England since about 1720. Harold and James Kirker go so far as to characterize the buildings of Boston from this period as "heavy dull houses indistinguishable from English models of half a century earlier." [19]

While Bulfinch saw many of the same monuments and buildings in Italy that had so influenced Adam, the most striking result for Bulfinch was to see first-hand the impact of those observations on the architecture Adam had designed for the city of London. Bulfinch hoped to introduce the Adam style to America, and to Boston in particular. The adherents of Adam's Neoclassicism "wanted to replace what they held to be the artificial vocabulary of Renaissance design with what they took to be the rational principles of pre-Roman building."[20] Archeological discoveries of the ancient Roman towns of Herculaneum and Pompeii, as well as the discovery of lost Greek temples at Paestum in southern Italy in the 1740s, had unearthed a whole new array of buildings that were

---

[16] Yarwood, 82.

[17] Yarwood, 108.

[18] Marcus Whiffen and Frederick Koeper, *American Architecture: Volume I – 1607-1860* (Cambridge, MA: The M.I.T. Press, 1983), 123.

[19] Harold Kirker and James Kirker, *Bulfinch's Boston 1787 – 1817* (New York: Oxford University Press, 1964), 31.

[20] Kirker and Kirker, 32.

vastly different from the villas and temples that English Palladianism was based on. These discoveries would initiate a rush of detailed archaeological study by English and German scholars. Delicate wall decorations and attenuated columns and proportions would replace what many considered to be the sterile and predictable forms of the Palladian Revival. Other exterior elements of the Federal, or Adam, style typically featured rectangular shaped buildings and facades, with low pitched roofs. Front doorways were often flanked by sidelights and were surmounted by a semicircular arched fanlight.

Interiors floor plans were affected as well. The typically square and rectangular rooms of the traditional hall-parlor floor plan would give way to rooms that could be circular or elliptical in shape. Moldings were finely executed, and ornaments were of a geometric nature.[21] In general, the details and ornament utilized by Adam were more delicate and refined than the details to be found on Georgian buildings based on the Palladian Revival.

While Bulfinch would spend the next several decades redefining the architectural landscape of Boston, his Neoclassical designs were much less influential in the rural areas west of Boston. Richard Cote reasoned that "since Boston contained the wealth, it would also contain the most accomplished craftsmen, and hence, the most innovative architectural trends."[22] If this was so, then how did Bulfinch's Neoclassical designs make their way to other regions such as the Connecticut River Valley?

Several aspiring builder-architects would move to Boston to learn about Neoclassical design from Bulfinch. Among the better known figures to come under Bulfinch's influence were Samuel McIntire (1757-1811) of Salem, and Asher Benjamin (1773-1845), who was born in Connecticut but had roamed throughout the Connecticut Valley for the first thirty years of his life.[23] McIntire's influence would be pervasive in Salem and on the seacoast of Massachusetts. His simple yet elegant Gardner-Pingree House in Salem is considered by many to be a masterpiece of Neoclassical design and execution (Fig. 8).

More importantly for Walpole and the inland communities of the

---

[21] Bryant Tolles, *New Hampshire Architecture: An Illustrated Guide* (Hanover, NH: University Press of New England, 1979), xx.

[22] Richard C. Cote, "Rethinking the Early Greek Revival: The Success of Influences and the Failure of a Builder," *Old-Time New England* Vol. LXIV: 66.

[23] Benjamin actually lived in Windsor, Vermont, from 1799 to 1802. Windsor is located just twenty miles or so north of Walpole. His time there was probably to oversee the building of a church and several houses in that community, and he began the first school for architecture in New England during his time in Windsor. There is no record of his ever having visited Walpole, though that is not out of the question.

Connecticut River Valley, Asher Benjamin would return to the region by 1803, where his architectural handbooks would be widely used by carpenters up and down the valley, from New Haven by the sea to the northern reaches of the upper Connecticut Valley in the town of Orford, New Hampshire. Benjamin's admiration for Bulfinch and his work is apparent, since he included in his 1806 edition of *The American Builder's Companion* an elevation (drawn by his co-author, Daniel Reynard) of Bulfinch's Boston branch of the Bank of the United States, which he designed in 1798 (Fig. 9).[24] Amazingly, this is the only detailed record of any of Bulfinch's many commercial structures.[25]

While Benjamin is credited with building a number of fine buildings throughout New England, his most important contribution to American (and Walpole) architecture are the handbooks, or builder's guides, that he wrote and published (see Appendix II for a complete listing of Benjamin's works). Benjamin had concluded that there was a need for someone to write these architectural guidebooks for American builders, since the English handbooks were expensive and excessively elaborate.[26] Benjamin's *The Country Builder's Assistant: Containing a Collection of New Designs of Carpentry and Architecture* (1797) is generally viewed as the first original treatise on architecture by an American.[27] William Hosley points out that, as early as July 24, 1798, this book was being advertised in *The Farmer's Weekly Museum*, a newspaper published and printed in Walpole by the shop of famed printer Isaiah Thomas (Fig. 10).[28] Other carpenter's handbooks, such as William Pain's *The Builder's Pocket Treasure,* and *The Practical Builder; or, Workman's General Assistant* were advertised and available as well. These, however, were Boston reprints of books by London architects.[29] Benjamin himself was immensely influenced by Pain's work. A look at Benjamin's books tells us that their primary use by builders was for details on things such as doorways, windows, and cornices, rather than the actual floor plans or structural designs. Indeed, freedom of plan was an important aspect of the emerging American style in

[24] Asher Benjamin, *The American Builder's Companion; or A New System of Architecture: Particularly Adapted to the Present Style of Building in America,* Plate 43 (Boston: Etheridge and Bliss, 1806), accessed May 25, 2017, http://digital.library.wisc.edu/1711.dl/DLDecArts.AsherBenj.

[25] Kirker and Kirker, 201.

[26] John Quinan, "Asher Benjamin as an Architect in Windsor, Vermont," *Vermont History* (Vol. 42 No. 3, Summer 1974), 184.

[27] William Morgan, introduction to the sixth edition (reprint) *The American Builder's Companion* by Asher Benjamin (New York: Dover Publications, 1969), vi.

[28] Hosley, "Architecture," 67.

[29] Hosley, "Architecture," 67.

FIG. 8 GARDNER-PINGREE HOUSE, SALEM by Samuel McIntire, 1805

FIG. 9 PLATE 18 BANK OF THE UNITED STATES, BOSTON by
Charles Bulfinch, 1798

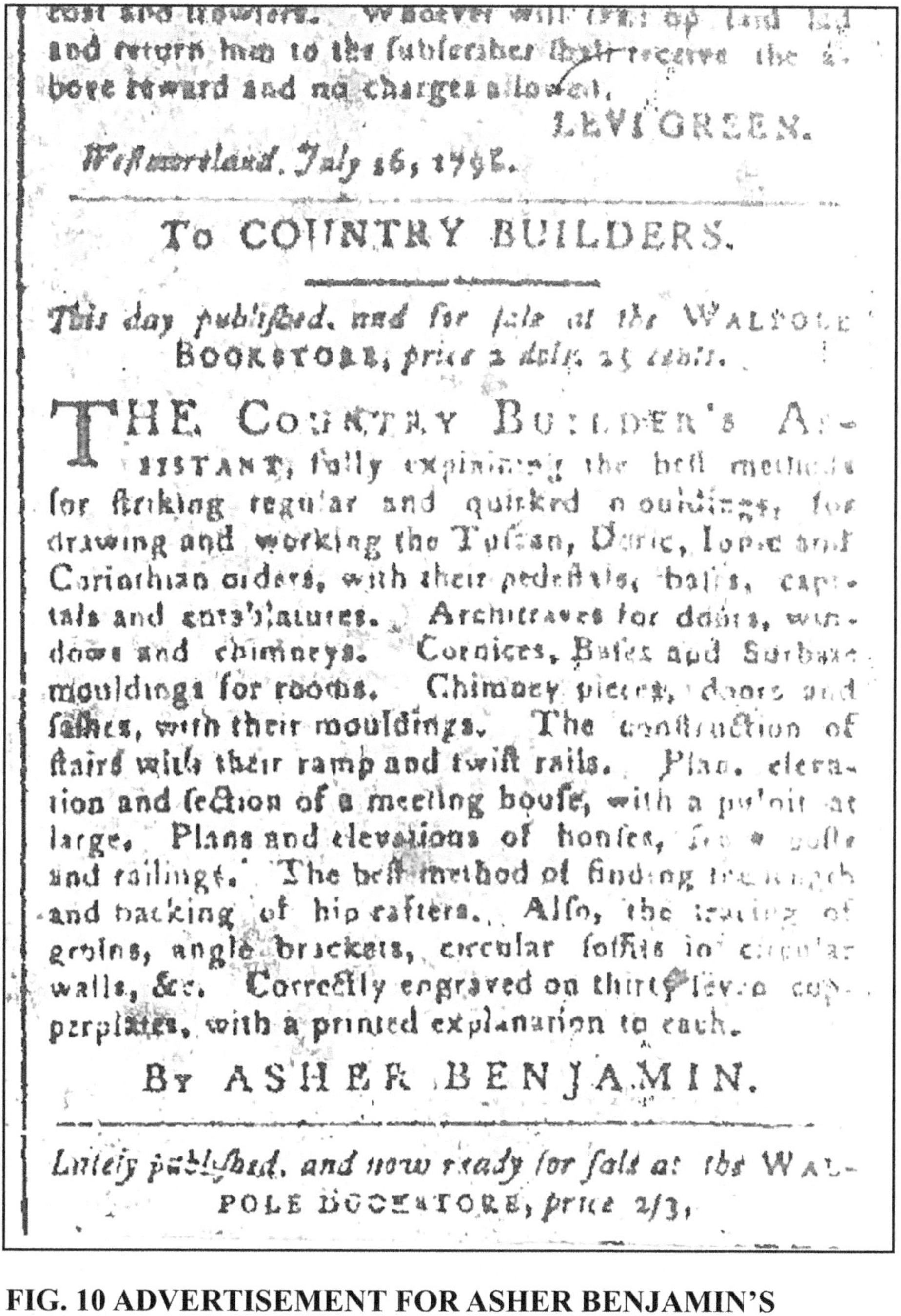

cost and trowlers. Whoever will take up said lad and return him to the subscriber shall receive the above reward and no charges allowed.

LEVI GREEN.

Westmorland, July 16, 1798.

To COUNTRY BUILDERS.

This day published, and for sale at the WALPOLE BOOKSTORE, *price 2 dols. 25 cents.*

THE COUNTRY BUILDER'S AS-SISTANT, fully explaining the best methods for striking regular and quirked mouldings, for drawing and working the Tuscan, Doric, Ionic and Corinthian orders, with their pedestals, bases, capitals and entablatures. Architraves for doors, windows and chimneys. Cornices, Bases and Surbase mouldings for rooms. Chimney pieces, doors and sashes, with their mouldings. The construction of stairs with their ramp and twist rails. Plan, elevation and section of a meeting house, with a pulpit at large. Plans and elevations of houses, &c. with bases and railings. The best method of finding the length and backing of hip rafters. Also, the tracing of groins, angle brackets, circular soffits in circular walls, &c. Correctly engraved on thirty seven copperplates, with a printed explanation to each.

By ASHER BENJAMIN.

Lately published, and now ready for sale at the WAL-POLE BOOKSTORE, *price 2/3,*

FIG. 10 ADVERTISEMENT FOR ASHER BENJAMIN'S CARPENTER'S GUIDEBOOK, *The Country Builder's Assistant* (1797) in The Farmer's Museum, Walpole, NH, July 24, 1798

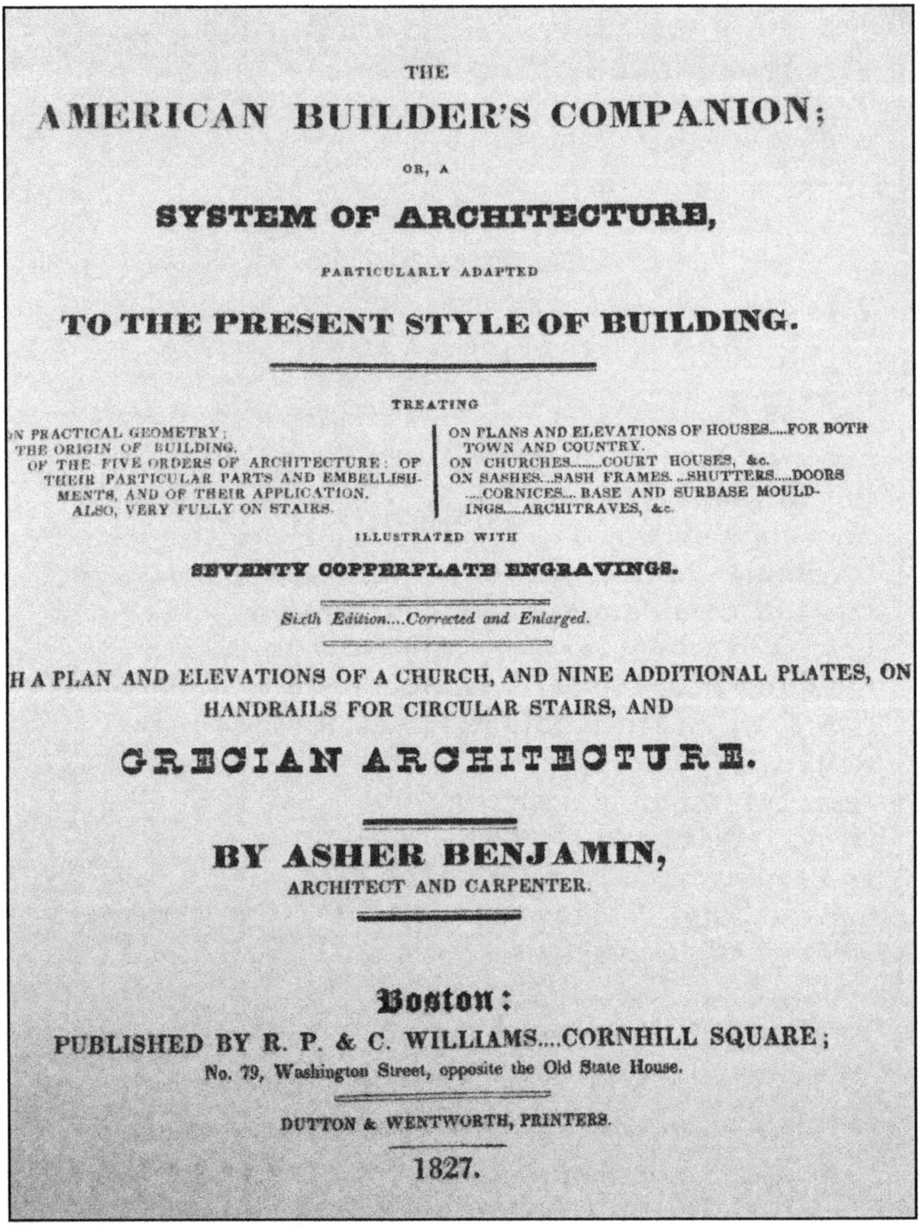

THE

AMERICAN BUILDER'S COMPANION;

OR, A

SYSTEM OF ARCHITECTURE,

PARTICULARLY ADAPTED

TO THE PRESENT STYLE OF BUILDING.

TREATING

ON PRACTICAL GEOMETRY ; THE ORIGIN OF BUILDING. OF THE FIVE ORDERS OF ARCHITECTURE : OF THEIR PARTICULAR PARTS AND EMBELLISH- MENTS, AND OF THEIR APPLICATION. ALSO, VERY FULLY ON STAIRS.	ON PLANS AND ELEVATIONS OF HOUSES.....FOR BOTH TOWN AND COUNTRY. ON CHURCHES.........COURT HOUSES, &c. ON SASHES...SASH FRAMES. ..SHUTTERS.....DOORS ....CORNICES... BASE AND SURBASE MOULD- INGS....ARCHITRAVES, &c.

ILLUSTRATED WITH

SEVENTY COPPERPLATE ENGRAVINGS.

Sixth Edition....Corrected and Enlarged.

H A PLAN AND ELEVATIONS OF A CHURCH, AND NINE ADDITIONAL PLATES, ON HANDRAILS FOR CIRCULAR STAIRS, AND

GRECIAN ARCHITECTURE.

BY ASHER BENJAMIN,

ARCHITECT AND CARPENTER.

Boston:

PUBLISHED BY R. P. & C. WILLIAMS....CORNHILL SQUARE;

No. 79, Washington Street, opposite the Old State House.

DUTTON & WENTWORTH, PRINTERS.

1827.

FIG. 11 FRONTISPIECE Asher Benjamin's *American Builder's Companion*, sixth ed. (1827). Note the sub-title advertising the addition of details on "Grecian Architecture"

architecture.

Since Benjamin's publication of his first book in 1797 precedes his time in Boston under the tutelage of Bulfinch, it's clear that he was already familiar with the English authors who were writing about and illustrating Neoclassical details in their own books.[30] This only served to whet his appetite to work directly with Bulfinch, who was transforming the city of Boston into a center of Federal architecture. Subsequent editions and works by Benjamin would reflect the new taste in architecture that he absorbed from working directly with Charles Bulfinch. In addition, his 1827 revised edition of *The American Builder's Companion* "offered the 'Grecian architecture' that was coming to replace the Federal style" (Fig. 11).[31] If these works were readily available through the local bookstore in Walpole, then clearly the means for local builders to utilize these guides for the purpose of building houses was available to them.

---

[30] In the Preface to the Sixth Edition of *The American Builder's Companion,* Benjamin acknowledges his debt to the English architect and mathematician Peter Nicholson. It's also likely that Benjamin was familiar with and borrowed extensively from William Pain's *The Practical Builder* (1774).

[31] Morgan, introduction, vii.

CHAPTER 3

Toward a National Architecture:
The Greek Revival

By 1820, the country was looking to create a truly national style of architecture. If the Federal Style was an example of a subtle attempt at establishing an American architectural style, "the Greek Revival was the first pervasive and self-conscious nationalistic movement in American architecture."[1] Indeed, the Greek temple would become the highest architectural ideal of Americans for more than a generation, lasting perhaps until about 1860.[2] Architectural historian Talbot Hamlin uses the story of the design and building of the Capitol building in Washington D.C. as a metaphor to explain the development of a distinctly American architecture:

> In the [building of the] United States Capitol, it required the careful and sympathetic administration of Bulfinch to accomplish this. Here one gets the real birth of American architecture, and here one finds a true expression of the definite character of the American Classic Revival, which out of so many diverse influences – from France and England, from Rome and Greece – but equally out of American conditions, out of American materials and ways of work, out of the very texture of American democracy, created a living architecture.[3]

Talbot seems to be saying that it's only fitting that a vast and diverse set of influences and people, such a hallmark of this country, had combined to create a uniquely American architecture, not the least of which were the "American

---

[1] Pierson, 432.

[2] Morrison, 575.

[3] Talbot Hamlin, *Greek Revival Architecture in America* (New York: Dover Publications, 1964), 44-45.

Table 3.1: Elements of Federal and Greek Revival Style, 1785-1850

Detail	Federal-Adamesque (1785-1820)	Greek Revival (1820-1850)
Facade	• Basic two story rectangular block • Symmetrically arranged chimneys (two or four) • Most often made of wood in New England • Plain exterior; sometimes included classical details such as semi-circular or elliptical fanlights over front entry • Palladian window often centered above front door • Elliptical entry porches	• Corners often marked by giant pilasters • Heavy entablature and full cornices • Symmetrical façade, though door is sometimes to one side; gable end forward • Full width porches supported by columns, typically in Greek orders (Doric, Ionic, Corinthian) • Palladian windows often centered above front door in pediment • Flush board siding
Doors	• Delicate, attenuated application of classical orders • Side pilasters as part of door surround • Side lights and elliptical light with lead muntins above door	• Elaborate door surround with sidelights and rectangular transom • Segmental pediment over door not uncommon
Roof	• Low pitched hipped or even flat roof, or side gables • Cornice with decorative molding	• Lower pitch gable roof most common • Gable end forward

Detail (cont.)	Federal-Adamesque (1785-1820) (cont.)	Greek Revival (1820-1850) (cont.)
Windows	• Double hung sash windows, usually six over six, separated by thin muntins • Windows arranged symmetrically, normally in five bays across the front • Plain or corniced windows • Single arched window on stair landing	• Dormers sometimes with arched windows • Typically six over six with larger panes and double hung sash • Pedimented windows
Interior Details	• Creative floor plans with elliptical, rounded rooms • Decorative ornament carved in wood or plaster moldings on walls, mantels, etc. • Curved, open staircases • Decorative motifs including swags, garlands, and urns	• Decorative ornament carved in wood or plaster moldings on walls, mantels, etc. • Curved, open staircases • Decorative motifs including swags, garlands, and urns

conditions, materials, and ways of work" he referred to. Furthermore, the Capitol was a monument to the diverse talents of several foreign architects,[4] but it was an American, Charles Bulfinch, who was able to pull these forces together into a cohesive and successful whole.[5]

Other factors contributed to the trend toward the Greek Revival as well. It didn't hurt that the Greeks were at that very moment in 1820 fighting their own war for independence from their centuries-old oppressors, the Turks, and that democracy had its origins in ancient Athens dating to the fifth-century B.C. Both of these factors allowed Americans to identify with the Greeks, and their

---

[4] Among the contributors were the Frenchmen Pierre L'Enfant and Stephen Hallet, the West Indian Dr. William Thornton, and the Englishmen George Hadfield and Benjamin Latrobe.

[5] Bulfinch would be the acting architect of the Capitol from 1817 until its completion in 1831. Talbot Hamlin seems convinced that, were Bulfinch not in charge, the project may never have come to a satisfactory conclusion.

temple architecture provided a means of expressing a set of values based on moral as well as political ideals. Virtue would be as valued as the aesthetics of a community's architecture.

In addition, the War of 1812 had forced many in America to conclude that they must make a final and total break with England. The Revolution of forty years earlier had severed political ties, but a sort of cultural dependence persisted. Departing from the Neoclassical style of Adam was but one more way of declaring America's independence from England. These circumstances were not lost on Americans who were celebrating their new modern democratic government. The romanticism of these events would heavily influence what Americans thought about the forces inspiring a new national identity through their architecture. By the middle of the century, another trend conjuring romantic ideas of style would emerge in the form of the Gothic Revival.

As was the case with the onset of the Federal style, there were many handbooks made available to builders. This became particularly so as new information was uncovered from the archaeological work being done in Italy and Greece. One of America's most influential architects of the nineteenth century was Ithiel Towne (1784–1844) of New Haven. He had a large library of material from which local architects could draw. Towne would later collaborate with Asher Benjamin to build a house in Northampton, Massachusetts. More locally, the previously mentioned handbooks of Benjamin would make a significant impact on building in the Connecticut Valley and Walpole. The sixth edition of Asher Benjamin's *The American Builder's Companion* (1827) would significantly include the addition of the Greek Orders and a host of details on Greek ornament.[6] The large number of Greek Revival buildings constructed in Walpole and throughout the region are clear evidence of Benjamin's impact.

The Greek Revival in New Hampshire frequently included a set of characteristics that anyone viewing the Athenian Parthenon atop the acropolis would understand. Greek structures were normally in the shape of a rectangular block, with a low pitched gable roof facing forward. Windows and doors were normally flat headed with heavy entablatures under the eaves. In addition, buildings were commonly painted white to simulate the marble of antiquity.[7] Within this general framework, we may also find elements of Federal style remaining on Walpole buildings generally thought to be Greek in style. Of

---

[6] Benjamin's *The Practical Builder* (1830) would also include this information. This turned out to be his most widely used handbook in the Connecticut Valley.

[7] Tolles, xxi. It should be noted that more recent archaeological research suggests that the ancient Greeks used brightly colored paint on their buildings (at least on entablatures) and statuary.

course, the most effective way to determine how these factors helped to shape the architecture of an eighteenth-century New England frontier town can be demonstrated by looking at the houses they left behind.

PART II

THE ARCHITECTURE OF WALPOLE

CHAPTER 4

From Georgian to Federal:
Walpole Architecture, 1790-1820

Located on Main Street is the Tatum-Peck House. This house, owned and probably built by Amasa Allen (1752-1821), was completed in 1792. He would live in this house until his death in 1821. Allen had come to Walpole from Pomfret, Connecticut in 1776 with little. However, he quickly established himself as a successful merchant in town, commencing business on the opposite side of Main Street, about 150 yards from where his house would one day sit. The name of his store was "Allen and Crafts," Joseph Crafts being a partner who came from Connecticut with him.

By 1792, Allen had established himself as a person of substance and means in Walpole. As evidence of Allen's elevated status in the town, only Benjamin Bellows purchased more pews in the new meetinghouse built on Prospect Hill in 1792. Allen purchased three, while five others purchased two, and thirty-five purchased one. Bellows purchased thirteen.[1] The purchase of even one pew would have signified a high degree of wealth and status in town. Allen would leave $75,000.00 to his heirs upon his death in 1821, an enormous fortune for the day.[2]

As might be expected, Amasa Allen was active in politics. He held many town offices, and from 1786 to 1791 served as the representative to the New Hampshire General Court. Later, in 1806, he served as a representative to the state legislature.[3] His stature in town then leads us to ask what his relationship may have been to the Bellows. Apparently, Allen and Bellows felt differently

[1] Frizzell, 652.
[2] Frizzell, 185.
[3] Frizzell, 658.

about at least one important issue: ratification of the Federal Constitution. Allen was an anti-Federalist and Bellows was in support of ratification. New Hampshire historian and scholar Jere Daniel reports that a search for the town's 1791 election records are mysteriously missing.[4] Had Bellows fixed the voting? We know that Allen served from 1786-91, but that it was Bellows who voted at the state ratifying convention. The truth may never be known, but it seems apparent that these two powerful individuals did not always agree.

With this kind of background, it isn't surprising that Allen would build a substantial residence for himself. The Tatum-Peck house (1791), as it has come to be known,[5] was indicative of the transitional state of architecture in country houses in the 1790s. The Tatum-Peck house demonstrates that country houses and their builders were not yet ready to let go of the Georgian past, yet they

FIG. 12 TATUM-PECK HOUSE, WALPOLE, unknown builder, owned by Amasa Allen, 1792

---

[4] This story comes by way of a lecture given by New Hampshire historian Jere Daniel in April 1988 to the Charlestown Historical Society. Records from before and after 1791 were present, while just those of 1791 were missing.

[5] The Tatum-Peck house is today named for long-time residents of the house in the twentieth century. The house is alternately known as the Amasa Allen house; Allen occupied the house for the first twenty-nine years of its existence until his death in 1821.

were flirting with details associated with the newer Federal style. The house is a two-story hipped-roof house with clapboard siding, corner quoining, and two chimneys with eight fire places (Fig. 12). The floor plan harkens back to the more typical Georgian layout, with a two-story central-hall plan and five-bay window facade facing forward.

This house also retains interior window shutters, a rather unique feature that appeared in more substantial houses in the eighteenth century. Architectural historian James Garvin attempts to correct a long held misconception regarding the purposes of this feature:

> Among the features that are often missing or damaged from eighteenth- or early nineteenth-century windows are interior shutters. Often mistakenly called Indian shutters, these features were not intended to defend a building against attack (for which they would have been useless) but to exclude the cold or to provide privacy in an age before window curtains were common.[6]

The shutters found in the Tatum-Peck house are of a type known as "sliding shutters" (Fig.13).[7] Garvin also points out that the paneling profile of the shutters, like so many other design aspects of this house, is of a typically Georgian style. The shutter would be fitted to slide behind the wall to be kept out of sight when not in use, and when needed could be slid into sight across the window. The style and technique utilized would be akin to construction of a "pocket door" today.

Although there are many houses of a similar style, the Tatum house seems richer in detail than most. The exterior features corner quoining, which, though not unknown in the Federal period, was a detail more commonly seen on mid-century Georgian houses. Indeed, most of the exterior details on this house are associated with the Georgian period. The cornice eaves are substantial, with a dentil range underneath

FIG. 13 TATUM-PECK HOUSE, WALPOLE, interior sliding shutter with characteristic Georgian paneling, 1792

---

[6] James L. Garvin, *A Building History of Northern New England,* (Hanover, NH: University Press of New England), 151.

[7] Garvin describes three types of interior shutters. Besides the sliding shutters described here, are types known as "hinged" and "folding" shutter, 151-152.

FIG. 14 BELLOWS-GRANT HOUSE, WALPOLE, Samuel Grant and unknown builder, 1792, remodeled c.1840. Note the extraordinary width of the house for a gable roof, as well as the later added giant corner pilasters

them. The windows have louvered shutters and the front door has a five light transom over it, cornice and dentil range matching that of the roof cornice. Doric pilasters flank the door as well.

While many of the characteristics and details of the house look back to the mid-eighteenth century, e.g., the double chimneys, corner quoining and central hall plan, the design, shape, and ornament reflects at least an awareness of, and desire to incorporate the newer designs of Robert Adam. A house of this magnitude would have been appropriate for a leading member of the community, and Amasa Allen certainly fit that description. Today, the house serves as the offices for Burdick's, a popular downtown restaurant located next to the Tatum-Peck house.

Diagonally across from the Tatum-Peck house on Main Street is the Bellows-Grant house. Constructed in 1792, it was originally built with both

FIG.15 BELLOWS-GRANT HOUSE,
WALPOLE, detail of front doorway

Georgian and Federal details, but was remodeled in the 1840s to include many Greek Revival details. This effort to update the house is evidenced by the broad gable that faces front, a feature of many Greek Revival buildings (Fig. 14). General Benjamin Bellows, the son of the founder and grantee of the town, had this house built as a wedding present for his daughter Phebe and his new son-in-law Samuel Grant. The house would actually be built by Grant.

There can be no doubt of the preeminent position of Benjamin Bellows in Walpole and in provincial and state affairs as well. Bellows held nearly all of the town offices at various times before and after serving in the Revolutionary War. An indication of the family's wealth and status by the 1790s is that Grant was forced to give up his own business of saddler to look after his wife's extensive holdings.[8] It would seem reasonable to believe that this house was built with the utmost consideration for taste and style.

The two and one-half story house was originally built with a low-pitched hipped roof. Of course, this was a detail associated with the late Georgian style that was prevalent in the year of its construction, 1792. The slate covered gable roof, along with other changes, was made by Samuel Grant's son George (his

FIG.16 DETAIL of fan light over the front door of the Bellows-Grant house

---

[8] Frizzell, 164.

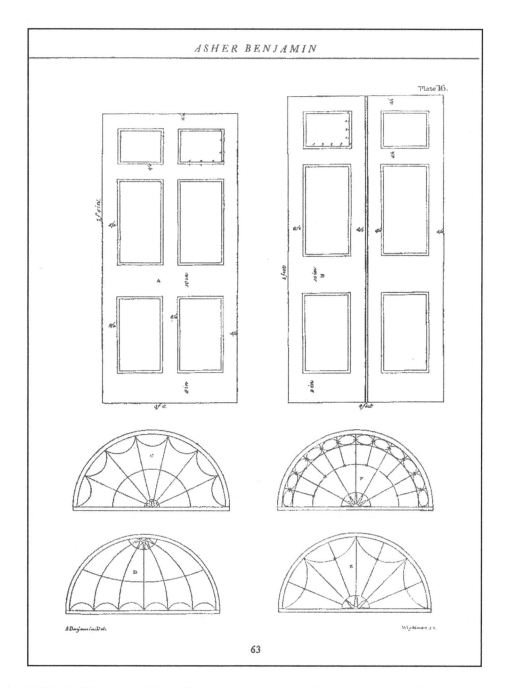

63

FIG.17 PLATE 17 Fan light design from Asher Benjamin's *The American Builder's Companion* (1806); likely inspiration for the fan light over the front door on the Bellows-Grant House

eighth offspring) in the 1840s. This, of course, coincided with the Greek style that was sweeping the Connecticut Valley and all of America by this time. The Georgian style doorway, with its triglyphs, triangular pediment, and dentil range suggest a more than modest attempt to bring a sense of high style and sophistication to the house (Fig. 15). The fan light design appears to have been taken from a plate appearing in an Asher Benjamin guidebook (Fig.16 and Fig.17).[9] The doorway on this house is arguably one of the most ornate and beautiful in town.

The sources for this door can be traced to the guidebooks of Asher Benjamin. Benjamin's inspiration for this doorway was likely the English author William Pain, a close follower of Robert Adam. Plate 12 in *The Country Builder's Assistant* (1797/1805) shows at least two examples (especially the figure on the right) of door designs remarkably similar to the doorway on this house (Fig. 18).[10] All the ornament around the door is aimed at meshing with the door itself to produce a sense of beauty and cohesiveness. The elegance of the doorway, which was normally centered in the facade of both Georgian and Federal period houses, was in the surround, or enframement of the door.[11] The interior of this house is of the typical central hall plan associated with the eighteenth century.

There are cornices over the first and third floor windows, a variation on the idea of alternating pediments to create a symmetrical effect. The rhythmic pattern can be stated as A – B – A, a technique often seen in the Adamesque mansions of Samuel McIntire's Salem.

Another striking feature of the house is its immense size, its façade spanning sixty feet. We should remind ourselves that this house was not built with the intention of having a gable roof spanning its façade. The corner Doric pilasters help to amplify this size, along with the prominent location the house occupies on Main Street. Its presence would have symbolized the dominant position of the Bellows family in Walpole. The building today houses the offices of LPL Financial.

---

[9] Asher Benjamin, *The American Builder's Companion; or A New System of Architecture: Particularly Adapted to the Present Style of Building in America* (Boston: Etheridge and Bliss, 1806) plate 16, accessed May 26, 2017, http://digital.library.wisc.edu/1711.dl/DLDecArts.AsherBenj

[10] Asher Benjamin, *The Country Builder's Assistant* (Greenfield, MA: Thomas Dickman, 1797), accessed May 28, 2017, https://openlibrary.org/books/OL15461586M/The_country_builder%27s_assistant

[11] Stanley Schuler, *Architectural Details from Old New England Homes* (West Chester, PA: Schiffer Publishing, 1987), 65.

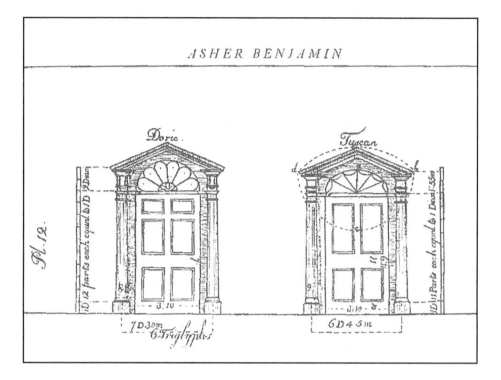

FIG. 18 PLATE 12 of Asher Benjamin's *The Country Builder's Assistant* (1805), possible source for the design of the door and surround on the Bellows-Grant house

The building that today serves as the clubhouse to the Hooper Golf Club was originally built as a tavern and inn. The builder and owner was Alexander Watkins. Watkins also worked as a tailor, but it isn't clear whether he gave up this trade when he built the tavern. Like Amasa Allen, Watkins had come to Walpole from Pomfret, Connecticut in 1777. After serving in the Revolutionary War, he apparently became a man of some means by the time he bought lot #4 in the 5th Range. He would have been thirty-seven years old when he built the tavern. He lived there with his wife Hannah until his death in 1824.

The house, which was built in 1792, appeared almost as it does today (Fig. 19). Although considered typical for the region, the most outstanding and unusual feature is the window and door quoining that accompanies the more typical corner quoining (Fig. 20). To the local craftsman, a sumptuous house without quoins would have been unthinkable (though never seen together with corner pilasters).[12] The addition of door and window quoining would have

---

[12] Pierson, 231.

FIG. 19 WATKINS TAVERN, WALPOLE, Alexander Watkins and unknown builder, 1792

been a deliberate attempt by Watkins to bring a greater degree of distinction to the house. Similar detail can be found on buildings of prominence in important coastal cities, including the Hancock House (1737) in Boston, and the Old Colonial Capitol Building (1739) in Newport, Rhode Island (Fig. 21).[13] Other more typical features include the hipped roof and clapboard siding. The front porch is original and features Doric columns supporting a rectangular portico. The side porches were added at a later date.

The floor plan is a central-hall type with stairs on the east. The pine floors, paneled doorways, and stairways are all original. There are two chimneys providing four fireplaces on each floor, with wainscoting wrapped around the chimneys.

The Tavern has been the center of much activity through the years. For a time, it was one of the favorite gathering spots of the "Society of Wits," a

[13] Pierson, 108 and Morrison, 481-82. Also known as the Colony House, the Newport building was designed by the builder/architect Richard Munday, and served as the state house for Rhode Island until 1901. Unfortunately, the Hancock house was demolished in 1863.

FIG. 20 WATKINS TAVERN, detail of unusual
quoining around windows and exterior doors

literary society formed around the turn of the nineteenth century. The place remained in the Watkins family until 1859 and eventually wound up in the possession of the Hoopers, an important Walpole family. George Hooper left the property to the town in 1909, which presently leases it to the Hooper Golf Club.

Legend has it that when Walpole resident Louisa May Alcott wrote her children's novel *Under the Lilacs* in 1878, she took the setting and inspiration for the story from the magnificent hedge of lilacs that grows along the bottom of Wentworth Road alongside the house known as the Knapp House (1812).[14] Apparently, Louisa May was a frequent visitor to this house during her several years residence in Walpole.[15] Built by Josiah Bellows, II, the grandson of Colonel Bellows, it was designed to be the most beautiful and imposing residence in town.[16] Arguably, Bellows accomplished his goal (Fig. 22). The Knapp house furnishes the purest example of the Federal style in Walpole.

Known locally as "Slick Si" because of his ability to talk so persuasively, Josiah Bellows was colorfully described as a "roistering gay blade about town."[17] The career of Bellows began as the owner and proprietor of a public house, i.e., a tavern. However, financial troubles forced him to mortgage the house. Considering the position of the Bellows family in the town, this must have been a great embarrassment for Josiah and his family. Perhaps this explains why he moved his family (including an African-American woman named Rachel, presumably a servant) further north to Lancaster, New Hampshire in 1824.

It seems clear that the house was fully intended to express a high degree of style and grace by its occupants. Even the location was chosen to make the house distinctive. Before the growth of trees obscured the view, one could stand at the upstairs hall window and look down onto the town's Main Street to view seven other houses of Bellows family ownership.[18] Except for the very bottom part of the road, present day Wentworth Road did not exist in the early nineteenth-century, so, along with another Bellows house directly across the street from it, the house would have stood alone in looking down on the village.

---

[14] This hedge of lilacs continues to perfume the houses and yards of lower Wentworth Road today.

[15] Marjorie W. Smith, *Historic Homes of Cheshire County, Vol. II* (Brattleboro, VT: Griswold Offset Printing, Inc., 1979), 147.

[16] Frizzell, 199.

[17] Smith, 147.

[18] Marjorie Smith, "Home of the Month: Walpole," *New Hampshire Profiles Magazine* (October 1968): 39-46.

FIG. 21 OLD COLONIAL CAPITOL BUILDING (COLONY HOUSE), NEWPORT, by Richard Munday, 1739. Note the quoining around the windows.

FIG. 22 KNAPP HOUSE, WALPOLE, unknown builder, 1812. Considered an example of a high style two-story brick Federal house

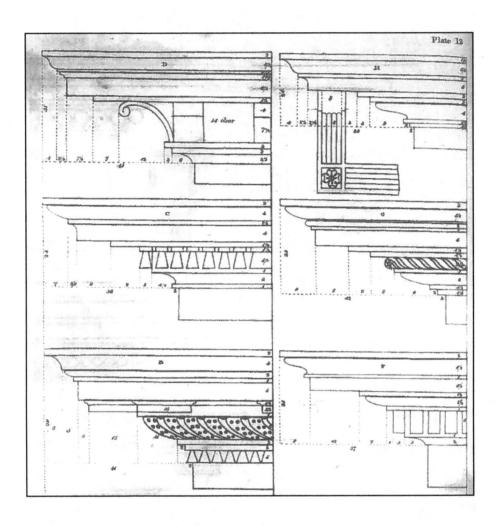

FIG. 23 ELEVATIONS Cornice design with guttae blocks and rope molding, from Asher Benjamin, *The American Builder's Companion*, 1806. Possible source for design on Knapp House

The house is a regionally typical example of a Federal style house, except that it is constructed of brick, a material more commonly associated with the Adam style in the southern part of the United States. In a region where wood was more typical due to its plenitude, this must have made the house stand out just that much more. Architectural historian James Garvin observes that the house possessed a degree of urbanity not commonly seen in country houses. He points out that "brick houses in New Hampshire outside of Portsmouth were rare until at least 1820."[19] In addition, Garvin attests that "the house shows the strong influence of architect and author Asher Benjamin."[20] The hip roof has a cornice with guttae blocks and rope molding, details very likely taken from an Asher Benjamin guidebook (Fig. 23).[21] The windows are all original (including some panes of glass) with louvered shutters, and have granite lintels with simulated double keystones,[22] a detail similarly found on Samuel McIntire's Gardner-Pingree house in Salem (Fig. 8). Interior details likely taken from Benjamin's guidebooks include the balustrade, which ends in a spiral, and the columns of the mantelpiece in the parlor, which rest on little balls.[23]

The plan of this house also reflects the Federal style. The chimneys are positioned away from the central portion of the house to the four corners. This arrangement opens up the interior, allowing for a greater utilization of space, and would likely have been considered superior stylistically.

The rectangular portico is supported by twin slender Tuscan columns on either side of a central entrance, and has an entablature with cornice and triglyphs along the frieze. This technique in effect "frames" the door when approached directly from the front. A single column provides support from the back. The projecting brick steps are elliptical in shape, as is the window above the door with its delicate tracery (Fig. 24). The elliptical shape of the portico steps echoes McIntire's Gardner-Pingree house (1805), though it is the covering portico rather than the steps which utilize this shape (Fig. 25). The door is original with three flanking side-lights.

An outstanding interior feature of the Knapp house is the original French

---

[19] Andi Axman, "Falling for a house" *New Hampshire Home* (May-June 2012) www.nhmagazine.com, (accessed May 30, 2017).

[20] Axman, "Falling for a house."

[21] Asher Benjamin, *The American Builder's Companion; or A New System of Architecture: Particularly Adapted to the Present Style of Building in America* (Boston: R.P. & C. Williams, 1806), accessed May 27, 2017, https://archive.org/details/americanbuilders00benj_0.

[22] Smith, *Historic Homes, Vol. II,* 148.

[23] Axman, "Falling for a house."

FIG. 24 KNAPP HOUSE ENTRANCE Note the elliptical brick steps, echoing the doorway portico to Samuel McIntire's Gardner-Pingree house in Salem

FIG. 25 GARDNER-PINGREE HOUSE ENTRANCE, SALEM
Larger, more ornate and highly embellished, but with similarities to the Knapp House. Its designer, Samuel McIntire, and Connecticut Valley builder (and author) Asher Benjamin, trained under the Boston builder and architect Charles Bulfinch

FIG. 26 KNAPP HOUSE, WALPOLE Detail of French Dufour
wallpaper "Monuments of Paris" in Knapp House

Dufour wallpaper, giving the house a refinement which must have been
very unusual in a rural house in the early nineteenth century. The wall paper
survives intact due to an extensive program of restoration (Fig. 26), and scenes
of "Monuments of Paris" remain in the northwest sector of the house, which is
used, perhaps fittingly, as a music room.[24]

The house was in Knapp family possession for over a century, hence its
name today, and reflects the attempt by the Bellows to elevate (or perhaps
live up to?) their name and status by building a house replete with the latest
architectural details and made with the most expensive materials. While not
anywhere near the size or scale of McIntire's masterpiece in Salem, the Knapp
house seems to express a conscious desire to build a house of elegance and
high style. The Knapp house is a fine example of a two-story brick Federal
house, built with many of the latest details coming to the Connecticut Valley
by way of Asher Benjamin's numerous carpenter's guidebooks.

---

[24] See: Andi Axman, "Falling for a house" for additional details on the restoration of
this extraordinary house.

CHAPTER 5

Aaron P. Howland, Master Builder of Walpole

In the first part of this essay, we traced the lineage and development of architectural style from its European origins to the urban centers along the coast of New England and finally to the inland areas of the Connecticut River Valley. However, we should be mindful that there was nothing inevitable about this process, and that this transmission of information was achieved by extraordinary people. Names like Palladio, Adam, Bulfinch, and Benjamin are easily found in the books that tell the history of architectural development in Europe, England, and America. However, the names that are just as important but less known to us are those of the dozens of master craftsmen and carpenter-builders throughout New England, the Connecticut Valley, and Walpole who actually utilized these guides to build the Georgian, Federal, and Greek Revival houses and buildings that give our communities their sense of character, style, and grace.

It seems that many communities had at least one significant carpenter-builder who is known to us today. In Walpole, the name of Aaron P. Howland (1801-67) dominates the period from about 1830 to roughly 1850 (Fig.27). The son of Charles Howland (reputedly a descendent of an indentured servant who came over on the *Mayflower*), Aaron had very little formal education and took it upon himself to learn his chosen trade of carpenter.[1] New Hampshire scholar Bryant Tolles describes Howland as a "gifted master builder."[2] In fact, Howland seemed to have had a hand in just about every significant structure built in Walpole during this period. It's also clear from the way Howland

---

[1] Much of the biographical material is from Ray Boas, "Aaron P. Howland," *As It Was…and Still Is…Walpole, New Hampshire* (Walpole, NH: Ray Boas, 2014), 102.
[2] Tolles, 153.

FIG. 27 Aaron P. Howland, builder-architect of Walpole, New Hampshire

applied ornament and detail that he was acutely aware of the latest architectural trends percolating in the 1830s and 40s, i.e., the Greek style and, later, the Gothic style. It's equally apparent that Howland was not afraid to stray from the guidebooks that were undoubtedly utilized to create his designs. With this said, there is clear evidence that Howland utilized the readily available guidebooks by Asher Benjamin to construct the various houses and buildings that are attributed to him.

Unfortunately, the names of master carpenters and builders from the earlier part of Walpole's history are harder to come by. Since Howland was born and raised in Walpole, it seems likely that he learned his trade from someone working in town. It's also probable that whoever trained Howland (perhaps there were several people who would contribute to his development) would have had access to and used the guidebooks of Asher Benjamin. These unknown carpenter-builders were responsible for the elegant Georgian and Federal style homes that remain in Walpole today. Since we know Walpole had a bookstore and print shop that sold the architectural handbooks authored by Asher Benjamin (and others) from the late 1790s onward, it's reasonable to conclude that guidebooks were being utilized by carpenters during the Federal period as well.

Born in 1801, Aaron Howland would have just been coming of age as a carpenter-builder as he approached his mid-twenties, thus coinciding almost perfectly with the emergence of the Greek Revival in the late 1820s. It shouldn't be a surprise then, that Howland had a hand in constructing most of the finest examples of Greek Revival homes and buildings in Walpole. In his award winning book *A Building History of Northern New England,* architectural historian James L. Garvin cites the Margaret Porter house (1790/1840) (Fig.28) on Main Street in Walpole as an illustration of the essence of the Greek Revival

FIG. 28 MARGARET PORTER HOUSE, WALPOLE, unknown builder, 1790, alterations 1837-40

FIG. 29 TEMPLE OF NEPTUNE, PAESTUM, ITALY, c. 450 BC.

in northern New England in general, and in Walpole in particular. Says Garvin, "In its most fully developed form, the Greek Revival house assumed the form of a classical temple."[3] The Temple of Neptune[4] (460 BC) in Paestum, Italy provides the prototype of the Greek temple in its purest original form, going back 2,500 years ago (Fig.29). In the fifth century BC, southern Italy was not yet part of the Roman world; instead, this region was part of "Magna Graecia" ("Greater Greece") at this early period, thus the presence of three great Greek temples on the plain of Paestum.

While the classical temple was the ideal, builders in the Greek Revival period would often feature details from an earlier period. Garvin points out that "…structures built during that period often show a combination of Federal and Greek Revival details."[5] For example, the previously cited Porter house features a louvered fan in the pediment, a detail more commonly associated with the earlier Federal style. While it's unclear what Howland's role may have

[3] Garvin, 115. It's probable, though not certain, that Aaron Howland was responsible for the alterations on the Porter house.

[4] Alternately referred to as the Temple of Hera.

[5] Garvin, 114.

been in the construction of the Porter house, both the purity of the classical temple, as well as the retention of Federal and Georgian details, were in evidence in the Greek Revival structures in Walpole. It's also clear that Aaron Howland was the primary practitioner of these principles throughout the town in the 1830s and 1840s, and may very well have directed the alterations on the Porter house.

CHAPTER 6

Triumph of the Greek Revival, 1820-1850

Any discussion of the Greek Revival in Walpole must begin with the aforementioned master builder Aaron Howland and the most iconic building in town, the Walpole Academy. Completed in 1831, its design and construction, like so many of the buildings constructed in Walpole from 1830 to 1850, was attributed to Howland. The building is situated on a knoll overlooking the downtown on Main Street, a subtle allusion to the heightened position of the Parthenon of Athens, as it overlooks the city atop the acropolis (Fig. 30).

The building has a well-proportioned four-column Doric portico, with a Federal style louvered fan centered in the flush board façade and pediment (Fig.31). The columns support a full entablature, with architrave, frieze decorated with triglyphs, and a cornice with dentils. The louvered fan is a detail leftover from the Neoclassical style that had dominated building for the previous thirty years in Walpole, and the cupola harkens back to an earlier time as well. While the Academy is overwhelmingly Greek in style and detail, like so many of Walpole's buildings, it features details from more than one architectural period. The building served as the town's high school until 1950, and today serves as the home of the Walpole Historical Society.[1]

Directly across from the Walpole Academy on Main Street sits the Buffum house. This house stands out as a home of great beauty and historical significance in Walpole. On first glance, one would have to question the construction date of 1785 for this obviously Greek Revival residence (Fig. 32). However, the house was indeed built in the Georgian style by Ebeneezer Crehore of Milton, Massachusetts.[2] How did a Georgian-style house built in

---

[1] Tolles, 155.

[2] Frank Roos, "Buffum House" *Historic American Buildings Survey*, 1959.

FIG. 30 WALPOLE ACADEMY by Aaron Howland, 1831

FIG. 31 WALPOLE ACADEMY, detail of portico, including fluted column, Doric capital, full Doric entablature with cornice, and flush board pediment with inset arched louvered fan.

FIG. 32 BUFFUM HOUSE, WALPOLE, Original construction by Ebeneezer Crehore, 1785; Aaron Howland alterations after 1835 changed the front of the house to Main Street

FIG. 33 BUFFUM HOUSE looking from north at original front of house, which was built in typical Georgian design, with centered door fronting on Middle Street

the eighteenth century come to epitomize the Greek Revival of the nineteenth? The answer to this puzzle lies with the major alterations made to the house in the 1830s.

Although Benjamin Bellows had the house built, some debate lingers regarding who the house was actually built for. Martha Frizzell says "There seems no reason why Bellows should have had such a house built. Did Crehore build it for himself and for some reason never receive title?"[3] Bellows would have been living across the street at the time in a house that no longer exists.

When the house was bought by David Carlisle in 1797, it had a hipped roof and was typically Georgian in style and detail.[4] Following several changes in ownership between 1802 and 1820, the house was sold to William Buffum, a well-known and prosperous merchant. The former home of the *Farmer's Weekly* would remain in possession of the Buffum family for the next 125 years. It was under Buffum's ownership that the house underwent major changes. It seems likely that the Buffums were anxious to express their own status by keeping up with the latest stylistic trend, and took steps to alter the house to reflect the Greek Revival that was sweeping the town and nation by the 1830s.

The similarity of the added portico to the one on the Walpole Academy suggests that Aaron Howland was responsible for the remodeling of the Buffum house.[5] Many details on the exterior were altered to create a house reflective of the Greek Revival, including the hipped roof that was changed to a gable roof. The original timbers in the attic are easily distinguished from the newer ones, since the originals are of oak, while those used for the alterations are of chestnut.[6] The two-story Doric portico which faces Main Street was originally a side of the house, which was first finished in the Federal-Georgian style. The front of the house originally faced north, onto Middle Street. The former front door was centered in the original five bay façade, and can still be observed with its pulvinated cushion frieze, a characteristic found on Federal doorways (Fig. 33).

The Main Street front, by contrast, reflects the country's changing architectural taste. Well-spaced columns support a full Doric cornice and entablature with triglyphs (Fig. 34). The pediment is of flush board, with a prominently centered Palladian window, and Doric pilasters are at the corners.

---

[3] Frizzell, 189.

[4] Marjorie Smith, "Home of the Month" *New Hampshire Profiles Magazine*, March 1966, 28.

[5] Tolles, 156.

[6] Smith, "Home of the Month," 28.

FIG. 34 BUFFUM HOUSE ENTABLATURE Detail of full Doric
entablature on the Buffum House

The front doorway has side-lights and a transom above, with leaded muntins
to divide the panes of glass. The first story windows are six over six with a
cornice, while the second and third story windows are twelve over twelve and
double hung.

The front door opens into a central hallway, which was remodeled
to accommodate the new front entrance. Paneling on the stair wall and an
elaborate balustrade adorn either side of the stairway.[7] These are the original
features of the house. Folding shutters appear all through the house on the
inside of windows and are also original.

On the other side of Middle Street but also facing Main Street, sits an
equally impressive Greek Revival house. This is the Porter house (Fig.28),
constructed in 1790 and redesigned in 1840. Together, these two houses make
for a handsome and dignified display of Greek Revival architecture on Main
Street in the center of town (Fig. 35). The Walpole Academy (Fig.30), located
directly across the street, completes an impressive triad of Greek temple
architecture that dominates the downtown.

The Bemis-Howland house (1833) was also built by the well-known local

---

[7] Smith, "Home of the Month," 29.

FIG. 35 BUFFUM HOUSE (1785/1835) AND PORTER HOUSE (1790/1840). Aaron Howland alterations on Buffum house, but author of Porter House alterations is less certain.

FIG. 36 BEMIS-HOWLAND HOUSE, WALPOLE, Aaron Howland, 1833

carpenter and craftsman Aaron Howland. The house sits at the head of the town common on Washington Square (Fig. 36). This house provides many examples of Greek Revival detail, while maintaining certain Federal elements as well. As is the case with so many other houses in town, it's certain that the handbooks of Asher Benjamin played a role in the details on this house.

Remarkably, this house had only five owners in the first 160 years of its existence, and today continues as a private residence. Howland built the house and apparently lived in it for nine years, since it was not sold until 1842. Otis Bardwell, a well-known local who controlled all the major stage routes in the vicinity until trains took over around 1850, bought the house from Howland. Bardwell's heirs sold to Alfred Burt in 1886, and in 1895 the house was sold to Jennie Spaulding before landing in the hands of "Mr. Walpole," Guy Bemis in 1938. Guy spent more than fifty years in the house, until his death in 1996.

The most obvious period details are the Palladian window[8] in the flush board pediment and the door surround, which is framed with pilasters and bull's eye corner blocks, and topped by a fret design commonly found in Greek decoration. This design was likely taken from Benjamin's guidebooks.[9] As is the case with most Greek Revival houses, the gable end of the house faces forward. The Victorian portico was added at a later date.

An interesting feature of the interior are the perforated heating tubes from the fireplaces. The idea was an attempt to disperse some of the heat generated by the fireplace throughout the house. The front parlor windows, which face south, have inside folding shutters (see chapter 4 for discussion of "sliding" interior shutters) which can be used to keep out summer sun or winter winds.[10]

It's not surprising that this house was not only built by a master builder such as Aaron Howland but that he would live in it himself. The construction of this house shows great concern for detail from both practical as well as aesthetic considerations. It's no wonder that Guy Bemis chose to stay so long in this house. Next door to the Bemis house is the Wing house, which features many similar architectural details. A major difference between the two houses is the Doric portico, which was added at a later time (Fig. 37). It seems very

---

[8] The Palladian window was a Georgian feature which increased in popularity during the Federal period. Though it had no real connection to Greek architecture, it was a frequently utilized detail on Greek Revival buildings.

[9] Asher Benjamin, *The Practical House Carpenter* (Boston: R.P. & C. Williams, 1843), accessed June 2, 2017, https://archive.org/details/architectorprac00benj.

[10] James Garvin claims that the folding shutters of the kind seen in the Bemis House are the rarest of the three types of interior shutters to be found in eighteenth- and nineteenth-century houses. Garvin, 151.

FIG. 37 WING HOUSE, WALPOLE Probably by Aaron Howland, 1840. This house, which resembles the Bemis House in numerous ways, sits next door to the Bemis-Howland house on Washington Square

FIG. 38 HOWLAND-SCHOFIELD HOUSE, WALPOLE, Gothic and Greek Revival details, Aaron Howland, 1844

(From American Builder's Companion)

FIG. 39 PLATE
from Asher Benjamin's
The Country Builder's
Companion (1806);
detail of Corinthian
capital design used on
Howland-Schofield
portico

FIG. 40 Detail of Corinthian capital on Howland-Schofield house
taken from Asher Benjamin design

FIG. 41 Detail of pointed arch Gothic pediments surmounting a row of windows on exterior of Howland-Schofield house

possible that the two houses were constructed by the same builder, which was of course Aaron Howland.

When Aaron Howland moved from his house on the common (the Bemis house), it was to move his family into the new house he was building on Elm Street around the corner. The Howland-Schofield house, as it came to be known, gave a hint of the stylistic changes that were in the wind by the 1840s. To this point, we've seen several examples of houses employing architectural details inspired by the Georgian, Federal, and the Greek Revival styles. In all cases, the architectural handbooks of Asher Benjamin were an important presence in the use of details for these styles.

The Howland-Schofield house (1844) would continue to employ details associated with the Greek Revival, but would also introduce features of the newest style to be seen in America, the Gothic Revival (Fig. 38). Many considered the Gothic to be a style employed strictly for ecclesiastical structures, but it was soon to be seen on domestic architecture, often in combination with classical details.

Mrs. Lucille Bragg offered testimony as to the reputation of Aaron Howland as a builder almost a century after construction of the house. Upon taking over the property in 1941, Mrs. Bragg said "The fact that the house was built by Aaron Howland for his own family undoubtedly accounted for its superior construction."[11] Mrs. Bragg was probably referring to the extra thick cellar and exterior walls, which are of brick covered with clapboards. The Greek

---

[11] Frizzell, 142.

Revival is represented by the Corinthian order columns of the east and west porticoes, with capitals of the type illustrated in a plate from Benjamin's *American Builder's Companion*[12] (Fig. 39 and Fig. 40), while the Gothic is represented by the pointed-arch louvered tops of the windows and dormers (Fig. 41). There are three dormers on both the east and west side of the steep, slate-covered gabled roof. The steepness of the roof line is yet another nod toward the Gothic, since Greek roof lines possess a shallower pitch.

Today the Howland-Schofield house functions as the offices and studio of Florentine Films, the company so well known for its documentary film making under the leadership of founder Ken Burns. The building itself is yet one more example of a transitional, or eclectic-style building in Walpole. Almost all the buildings cited in this essay possess a primary style, but retain details from a prior age, or, as in the case of the Howland-Schofield house, even look ahead to the future.

---

[12] Asher Benjamin, *The Country Builder's Assistant*, 17.

EPILOGUE

There seems to be little doubt that Walpole's architecture was utilized by its citizens as a way of indicating their desire to elevate themselves socially and, in some cases, politically. The most prosperous families of Walpole selected lots which would prominently display their wealth and status, which could be best illustrated by the house they lived in. The most prominent of all families were the Bellows, and they did not hesitate to assert their high-ranking position through the numerous mansions they built for themselves in and around Walpole village.

The style and taste of these houses was often dictated by the trends in design which had their origins in Europe, the prosperous seacoast communities of New England, and eventually the inland communities of the Connecticut River Valley. This process of transmitting information and style was carried to America in several different ways, including drawings, sketches, and in some cases, via the memory of those who traveled on the Grand Tour. But mostly this information came to New England and the Connecticut River Valley via architectural handbooks. The Boston architect Charles Bulfinch provides the background for the connection between coastal New England and the inland region of the Connecticut Valley in the early nineteenth-century.

Upon returning from his European tour in 1786, Bulfinch provided the most important and direct source of inspiration for the Adam style in Boston and then New England. Since both Connecticut Valley author and architect Asher Benjamin and Salem master builder and carver Samuel McIntire worked for a time under Bulfinch, some common details and techniques can be seen in the work of McIntire in Salem and the houses built from Benjamin's guidebooks in the Connecticut Valley. Though the work of McIntire was clearly more "high style" than even the finest houses in Walpole, this disparity was inevitable given the economic and physical limits that builders in Walpole had to contend with.

FIG. 42 ROENTSCH HOUSE, WALPOLE, Colonial Revival mansion built in the Palladian style with two story Corinthian portico, 1915

Though Salem was a prosperous and urbane coastal community and Walpole a rural community on the edge of the frontier, some commonalities of design have been pointed out between the work of McIntire in Salem and houses that were clearly influenced by the guidebooks of Asher Benjamin in Walpole. However, it's been made clear that local builders and craftsmen, such as Walpole's Aaron Howland, did not hesitate to veer from the dictums of the designs that existed in these guidebooks. Owners and builders applied their own taste and judgement in deciding what their houses and buildings would ultimately look like. While Howland utilized these guidebooks, we know he constantly added to and varied the designs and details found in those books, making for an architecture which was unique, eclectic, and constantly changing. Aaron Howland built many fine buildings, not only in Walpole but in surrounding communities as well.

After 1850, the nation would see a multitude of architectural revivals, and Walpole was not immune to these emerging changes in style and taste. Revivalism of one sort or another would characterize American architecture for the next century, with Gothic, Italianate, and Romanesque revivals making their appearance in the second half of the nineteenth century. However, the Neoclassical Revival, even in its variety of adulterated (and some would say debased) forms, would endure as a style preferred by many Americans throughout the late nineteenth and early twentieth centuries. Perhaps the grandest example in Walpole of the mania for the Neoclassical Revival is embodied in the Roentsch house (1915), an imposing Palladian mansion complete with a Corinthian order two-story classical portico (Fig.42). Many architectural historians lament that the builders of these houses were not always terribly concerned with the accurate replication of period details or the proportions associated with eighteenth-century houses.[1]

The people of Walpole have saved an impressive number of homes from the town's earliest period of settlement. Many that were in disrepair some years ago have been restored, often to near original condition and appearance. The architecture of the town is one way the people have been able to maintain their heritage, for the buildings which survive from the past are a fascinating reflection of the people who built and lived in them.

[1] Baker, 86.

ACKNOWLEDGMENTS

I am grateful to all those who assisted and advised me in the writing and creation of this book. In no particular order, my gratitude goes out to:

Mark Wojchick and Allura Lincoln, whose expertise and advice helped to create the beautiful and clear photographs in this book.

Connie Burns and Alicia Burns for their thorough and professional review of the manuscript, as well as their editorial suggestions. Their knowledge and expertise made the final manuscript a stronger and more convincing read.

In addition to individuals, several institutions provided help and assistance over the course of my research and writing. The staffs of both the New Hampshire Historical Society, and the New Hampshire State Library helped direct me to resources and information that contributed greatly to the final manuscript. Both institutions are located in the state's capital city of Concord. Also, thanks go out to the Walpole Historical Society for granting me access to the resources of the WHS.

Thank you to Bill Doreski of Keene State College, who many years ago launched my interest in local architecture when I was a student of his in graduate school.

Finally, thank you to my wife Lisa for her unswerving support, as well as the occasional technical assistance that was needed along the way.

PHOTO CREDITS

All photographs, except for those noted below, are by the author.
Photographs by Mark Wojchick: Figures 12, 15, 19, 20, 22, 28, 30, 31, 32, 33, 34, 37, 38, 40, 41

Historic American Buildings Survey (1959), Ned Goode, Photographer: Figures 13, 24, 26

From: George Aldrich, *Walpole As it Was and As It Is,* opposite page 307, Figure 27

Front cover, bottom: Painting *Village School House and Academy Building, Walpole, New Hampshire,* Mary A. Read, 1854 (collection of Walpole Historical Society)

Top left: Front door and surround, Bemis house (author photo)
Top right: Original sign, *Watkins Tavern,* 1795 (collection of Walpole Historical Society)

GLOSSARY OF ARCHITECTURAL TERMS

Architrave – Lowest of the three divisions of the entablature.

Capital – The top part of a column. Each of the five orders (Doric, Ionic, Corinthian, Tuscan, and Composite) has its own design.

Composite Order – This order combines features of the Ionic and the Corinthian orders.

Corinthian Order – The most elaborate of the three Greek orders, the order was reputedly inspired by the sight of a basket of toys placed on the grave of a Corinthian girl, around which wild acanthus had grown.

Cornice – The uppermost of the three sections of the entablature. This section often protruded to form a "shelf" for decoration or statuary, as well as to protect inhabitants from falling rain.

Dentils – Small, closely-spaced blocks placed along the bottom of a cornice.

Doric Order – The oldest and simplest of the Greek orders. This order, unlike the Ionic and Corinthian, has no base and normally employs fluting. The capital consists of a plain rounded disc that sits atop the column and below the architrave.

Entablature – The horizontal bands of decoration supported by the columns. The three parts, from bottom to top, are the architrave, frieze, and cornice.

Fluting – Vertical channels carved into the column. Most often found in the Doric order, never in the Tuscan, and sometimes in the others.

Fret – A geometric design of vertical and horizontal lines, such as the Greek key pattern.

Frieze – The middle section of the three divisions of the entablature. This section is often decorated with triglyphs, metopes, or other relief sculpture.

Guttae Blocks – Small conical pieces carved on the architrave, and below the cornice.

Ionic Order – This order is distinguished by its use of volutes.

Keystone – The central stone at the summit of an arch, locking the entire structure together.

Lintel – The horizontal support, normally of wood or stone, across the top of a door or window.

Metope – Space between sections of triglyphs on the frieze; often decorated with relief sculpture of some kind.

Muntin – A bar of supporting strip between adjacent panes of glass, often found in fan or side lights above and beside entrance doors.

Order – The total assemblage of parts comprising the column, capital, and its appropriate entablature.

Palladian – Motif based on the design of the sixteenth-century Italian architect Andrea Palladio. Principally, the concept includes an arch held up by columns. This concept serves as the basis for the "Palladian Window," sometimes referred to as a "Venetian Window."

Pediment – A triangular space created by sloping eaves and a horizontal cornice; may surmount doorways or windows, or serve as the frame of a gable. Variations of the triangular pediment include the segmental and broken pediment.

Pilaster – The representation of a column for decorative purposes, normally around doorways, but also found in interiors or in larger scale on the façade and corners of buildings.

Portico – A sheltered structure for walking under, usually applied to the columned projection to a Greek temple.

Pulvinated – A section of the frieze that is curved, usually in a convex shape; sometimes called "pulvino."

Quoins – The decorative angles normally seen on the corner of buildings, and more rarely, on windows and doorways.

Rustication – Imitation of masonry, frequently found on buildings of wood in New England to imitate the stone or marble of antiquity.

Swag – A molding or carving shaped as a decorative garland or chain of flowers, foliage, or fruit; commonly seen on fireplace mantels or a frieze.

Triglyph – A feature most often seen in use with the Doric order; consisting of groups of three vertical relief columns spaced evenly along the frieze.

Tuscan Order – Deriving from a Roman style temple; similar to the Doric, though with less ornament and without the fluting common to the Doric order.

Volute – Scrolled or coiled ends of a design element inserted into the capital of the Ionic order.

APPENDIX I

Select List of Architectural Handbooks Commonly Used in Colonial America

(I)   **Books Emphasizing Renaissance/Palladian Architectural Theory:**

Andrea Palladio, *Four Books of Architecture,* first of fourteen editions in 1663.
Colen Campbell, *Vitruvius Britannicus,* 1715.
William Kent. *Designs of Inigo Jones,* 1727.
James Gibbs, *A Book of Architecture,* 1728.
Isaac Ware, *Designs of Inigo Jones,* 1735.
William Adam, *Vitruvius Scoticus,* 1750.

(II)   **Carpenter's Handbooks Widely Used in the Colonies:**

Batty Langley, *The City and Country Builder's and Workman's Treasury of Designs,* 1740.
Batty Langley, *The Builder's Jewel,* 1741.
William Halfpenny, *The Modern Builder's Assistant,* 1742.
Abraham Swan, *British Architect,* 1745.
Robert Morris, *Rural Architecture,* 1750.
Robert Morris, *Select Architecture,* 1757.
William Pain, *The Practical Builder.* 1774.

From: Hugh Morrison, "Emergence of Georgian," *Early American Architecture,* 1987, 290-91.

The "Carpenter's Handbooks" (group II) were created as inexpensive alternatives to the large and expensive books and folios in the first group. Because of their low cost and portability, the books in the bottom group were much more widely used by builders in eighteenth-century New England. Thomas Jefferson was reputed to have used Robert Morris's *Select Architecture* extensively in the design and building of Monticello in Virginia.

APPENDIX II

List of Guidebooks Written and Published by Asher Benjamin

The Country Builder's Assistant, 1797.
The American Builder's Companion (with Daniel Reynard), 1806.
The Rudiments of Architecture, 1814.
The Architect, or, Practical House Carpenter, 1830.
The Practice of Architecture, 1833.
The Builder's Guide, 1838.
The Elements of Architecture, 1843.

These books were revised and reissued in forty-five editions, mostly in Benjamin's lifetime

APPENDIX III

A Brief Timeline of Early New England Architecture
1600 - 1850

1600	**COLONIAL PERIOD (1600-1780)**
	FIRST PERIOD ARCHITECTURE (1600-1715)
1650	
1700	
	SECOND PERIOD ARCHITECTURE (1715-1785)
	Georgian Style:
	Early Georgian (1715-1750)
	High/Late Georgian (1750-1790)
1750	
	EARLY NATIONAL PERIOD (1785-1830)
	Federal/Adam Style (1785-1830)
1800	
	NATIONAL PERIOD (1820-1860)
	Greek Revival Style (1820-1850)
	Gothic Revival Style (1840-1860)

APPENDIX IV

A fair copy transcription of Asher Benjamin's advertisement for his book *The Country Builder's Assistant,* found in the July 24, 1798 issue of *The Farmer's Weekly Museum*

To COUNTRY BUILDERS

This day published, and for sale at the WALPOLE BOOKSTORE, *price and deliv. 25 cents.*

The Country Builder's Assistant, fully
explaining the best methods for working regular
and quirked moldings, for drawing and working
the Tuscan, Doric, Ionic, and Corinthian orders,
with their pedestals, bases, capitals and entablatures.
Architraves for doors, windows and chimneys. Cornices,
-------, and --------- moldings for rooms. Chimney pieces,
doors and stairs, with their moldings. The construction
of stairs with their ramp and twist rails. Plan, elevation
and section of a meeting house, with a pulpit at large.
Plans and elevations of houses, -------- and railings. The
best method of finding the length and backing of hip
rafters. Also, the tracking of groins, angle brackets, circular
soffits in circular walls, & so on. Correctly engraved on thirty
------- copperplate, with a printed explanation to each.

By Asher Benjamin

Lately published, and now ready for sale at the WAL-
POLE BOOKSTORE, *price 2/3*

BIBLIOGRAPHY

Books and Printed Sources

Aldrich, George. *Walpole As It Was and As It Is*. Claremont, NH: Claremont Manufacturing Co., 1880.

Baker, James Milne. *American House Styles: A Concise Guide*. New York: The Countryman Press, W.W. Norton and Company, Inc., 2018.

Behrendt, Michael. *The Architectural Jewels of Rochester, New Hampshire: A History of the Built Environment*. Charleston, South Carolina: The History Press, 2009.

Benjamin, Asher. *Practice of Architecture* and *The Builder's Guide*. New York: DaCapo Press, 1994. (Reprint edition of original editions, 1839 and 1845)

Benjamin, Asher. *The American Builder's Companion*. New York: Dover Publications, 1969. (Reprint edition of the sixth edition of 1827)

Boas, Ray. *As It Was...and Still Is...Walpole, New Hampshire*. Walpole, New Hampshire, 2014.

Bridenbaugh, Carl. *Peter Harrison: First American Architect*. Chapel Hill: University of North Carolina Press, 1949.

Chamberlain, Samuel. *A Small House in the Sun: The Visage of Rural New England in Photographs*. New York: Hastings House, 1971. (Reprint of the 1936 first edition)

Downing, Andrew Jackson. *The Architecture of Country Houses*. New York: Dover Publications, Inc., 1969. (Reprint of original 1850 publication)

Ellis, Harold Milton. *Joseph Dennie and His Circle*. Austin: University of Texas, 1915.

Frizzell, Martha. *A History of Walpole, New Hampshire, Vol. I*. The Vermont Printing Co., 1963.

Garvin, James L. *A Building History of Northern New England*. Hanover, NH: University Press of New England, 2001.

Hamlin, Talbot. *Greek Revival Architecture in America*. New York: Dover Publications, 1964.

Heffernan, Nancy Coffey and Ann Page Stecker. *New Hampshire: Crosscurrents in Its Development.* Grantham, New Hampshire: Tompson and Ruuter Inc., 1986.

Hosley, William N. "Architecture." In *The Great River: Art and Society of the Connecticut Valley, 1635-1820,* edited by Gerald W.R. Ward and William N. Hosley, 63-133, Hartford, CN: Wadsworth Museum, 1985.

Kirker, Harold and James Kirker. *Bulfinch's Boston 1787-1817.* New York: Oxford University Press, 1964.

Morrison, Hugh. *Early American Architecture: From the First Settlements to the National Period.* New York: Dover Publications, 1987.

Pierson, William H. *American Buildings and Their Architects – Volume I: The Colonial and Neoclassical Styles.* New York: Oxford University Press, 1986.

Roos, Frank. *Historic American Buildings Survey.* 1959.

Schuler, Stanley. *Architectural Details from Old New England Homes.* West Chester, PA: Schiffer Pub., 1987.

Smith, Marjorie W. *Historic Homes of Cheshire County, Vol. II.* Brattleboro, VT: Griswold Offset Printing, Inc., 1979.

Summerson, John. *The Classical Language of Architecture.* Cambridge: The M.I.T. Press, 1983.

Tolles, Bryant. *New Hampshire Architecture: An Illustrated Guide.* Hanover, NH: University Press of New England, 1979.

Wheelwright, Thea and Katherine Knowles. *Travels in New England.* New York: Bonanza Books, 1989.

Whiffen, Marcus and Frederick Koeper. *American Architecture: Volume I – 1607-1860.* Cambridge, MA: MIT. Press, 1983.

Yarwood, Doreen. *Robert Adam.* New York: Charles Scribner's Sons, 1970.

Journals and Periodicals

Boas, Ray. "Did You Know That…? Excursions into Walpole People, Places & History with Ray Boas." *The Walpole Clarion,* Vol. VIII, Issue 5,

April, 2018.

Cote, Richard C. "Rethinking the Early Greek Revival: The Success of Influences and the Failure of a Builder." *Old-Time New England,* Vol. LXIV: 66.

No author. "Historic American Buildings Survey." *Historical New Hampshire*, Vol. XVIII, No. 2: 16-17.

Quinan, John. "Asher Benjamin as an Architect in Windsor, Vermont." *Vermont History,* Vol. 42, No. 3, Summer, 1974: 184.

Reinhardt, Elizabeth and Anne A. Grady. "Asher Benjamin in East Lexington, Massachusetts." *Old-Time New England* Vol. LXVII: 23-35.

Smith, Marjorie. "Home of the Month: Walpole" *New Hampshire Profiles Magazine* (October, 1968), 39-46.

Smith, Marjorie. "Home of the Month" *New Hampshire Profiles Magazine* (March, 1966), 28.

Online Sources

Axman, Andi. "Falling for a house." *New Hampshire Home* (May-June 2012): Accessed May 30, 2017. http://www.nhhomemagazine.com/May-June-2012/Falling-for-a-house/

Benjamin, Asher. *The American Builder's Companion; or A New System of Architecture: Particularly Adapted to the Present Style of Building in America.* Boston: Etheridge and Bliss, 1806. Accessed May 26, 2017. http://digital.library.wisc.edu/1711.dl/DLDecArts.AsherBenj

Benjamin, Asher. *The Country Builder's Assistant.* Greenfield, MA: Thomas Dickman, 1797. Accessed May 28, 2017, https://openlibrary.org/books/OL15461586M/The_country_builder%27s_assistant

Benjamin, Asher. *The Practical House Carpenter.* Boston: R.P. and C. Williams, 1843. Accessed June 2, 2017. https://archive.org/details/architectorprac00benj.

Wentworth, Bruce. "Ask the Architect: 'Federal.'" *Ask the Architect*: www.Askthearchitect.org accessed May 24, 2017.

Made in the USA
Middletown, DE
09 February 2019